Gourd Seed

Gourd Seed

Coleman Barks

MAYPOP BOOKS   Athens, Georgia

Cover: Corona Imperialis Polyanthos, reproduced from December 1989 of the Georgi calendar, "The Garden of Eichstaett," by permission of Verlag Dr. Rudolf Georgi, Aachen, Germany, and Georgi Publishers, Box 6059, Chelsea, MA 02150.

ISBN 0-9618916-6-1

Acknowledgements:
Agni—"Bedclothes"
Harvard Quarterly—"We Have Written Out Our Dreams"
Poetry Miscellany—"Fried Green Tomato Sandwiches," "A Section of the
    Oconee Near Watkinsville"
New Virginia Review—"Titty-Bream," "Spectacles," "Becoming Milton"
Plainsong—"Summer Food," "Each Peach," "The Problem," "New Year's
    Day Nap," "The Restaurant Woman," "The Grocery Store," "This,"
    "Spring Lizards," "Soft Applause," "The Fire"
Georgia Review—"Fivepoints," "In the Woods, You and I"
Quarterly Review—"WRFC"
Ironwood—"The Tree"
Chattahoochee Review—"Let the Door Be Locked," "Nightwork"
Memphis State Review—"Hymenoptera"
Painted Bride Quarterly—"Some Orange Juice," "Vigil Notes"
Kenyon Review—"Small Talk"
Zone 3—"A Walk in the Botanical Gardens," "Green Rocks," "A Wish,"
    "Kindling"
Southern Poetry Review—"The Great Blue Heron," Winner of the
    Guy Owen Poetry Prize, 1986. William Matthews, judge.
Poetry East—"Higdon Cove"
New England Review / Breadloaf Quarterly—"Carolina Silverbells,"
    "The Premise," Winner of NEQ/BLQ Narrative Poem Contest, 1987.
    Tess Gallagher, judge.
Chouteau Review—"Rained In, Nursing Unacted Desires"
Epos—"The Brain-House," "Tu Fu Rephrased, and Kittsu"

for Benjamin and Cole

Contents

A Wish

I love the microphone breath-flutter,
the famousness of words, that keeps me up late
and remote from a cigar-sweet closet
under the stairs where an old man
reads his Bible and hears the encores
and turns out the overhead to nap,
with applause so softened and made
whole by the basement walls.

Deep Sleep is his name, and just by not dying,
he refreshes, as dawns have my life so rarely,
though now less rarely. More often,
he talks and walks me through the scripture
of aching light, the way he's hoped he could.

A Section of the Oconee Near Watkinsville

Before I get in,
the aluminum canoe floats flat on the shine
of water. Then I ruin its poise.
Middle of the first shoal though, I'm out,
stumbling through the ankle-breaking rocks.
Canoe free-floating downstream, without decision
or paddle. I lunge and bruise across the shallows
to get a forefinger in the rope eye on the stern.

June afternoon light. June afternoon water.

I know there's a life being led in lightness,
out of my reach and discipline.
I keep trying to climb in its words,
and so unbalance us both.
The teacher's example is everywhere open,
like a boat never tied up, no one in it,
that drifts day and night, metallic dragonfly
above the sunken log.

Buttermilk

These flowers outlast
the houses they delight
to walk out from in thin Spring dresses
to where relatives used to live, when they were new lovers,
with now cedar trees growing through the bedsprings
by the three grey stone steps that lead nowhere.

The brain-bulbs twin and quadruple
in the translucent ground.

And whatever we say or do is a new clove
on the cluster we're with,
that helps the cup-shapes come up,

that have no use I know of,
except to hold your cheek close
and let someone see if it reflects,
which tells if you love
buttermilk or not.

Or maybe that was just the ending
our family had for the ritual.
I have never even liked buttermilk,
though I've not tried it for forty years.

I shall taste again, I promise
into these frilly, old-fashioned telephones
that stand here without their ear-pieces,

what my father never understood
why nobody else but him enjoyed,
the bitter breast,
that left a froth of surf-lines
in his ordinary glass.

The House of the Tibetan Bellmaker

Down off a steep-hanging Darjeeling
mountainside my feet fumble
a stairstep path through bare, tin
shacks. Bare, outside.
What we enter is a marriage,
shining with dark wood and candles
and silver bowls of springwater
and fresh tanka paintings, fierce blue,
life-changing males, and the green woman.

Each bell has gender. I tell my visitors
to close their eyes, now clear
on the other side of this elaborate planet
and lightly waggle to let them guess.
Sweet gossip.
        One of the beautiful—early
twenties—daughters has her brother
tell my friend she likes me.
        O talk more,
metallurgy. How resonating absorbs
and gives back a wave-weaving
from a center as it receives
the other.
        I want to love you
in that precarious town pitched
on the spine of a Himalayan ridge.

I want an inwardness
that's nothing familiar,
a rosy, tea-colored sky
moving like shelter,
in balance.

Higdon Cove

Give it the next fellow.
Not the ten dollars, the help. No mistaking
what he meant or saw the afternoon as,
a fine chance. The 1965 tractor started up,
though one of its brakes kept sticking, amusing him.
I'd gotten as far as I could trying to find a new walk,
to a gate bar across the road and backed back and onto
soft shoulder, slid helplessly into the ditch, hopeless
to maneuver out of. Walked to the nearest house.
He came to the door still chewing his lunch,
then toward the barn, I making polite apology.
You're heading for that tractor, aren't you?
If it won't start, we'll get a horse.
The man who wants no credit, or even to shake hands,
too busy with what needs doing, holds his arms
close in and sidles by me in the barn
like I'm a ticklish passage, me holding out my money.
Give it the next fellow.

There is a huge holly tree next to where I glided to a stop,
a solid thigh-trunk white-splotched
and stretching deep under the ditchwater.
Beauty, but not such as this man is,
beyond any tree.

The Great Blue Heron

Flying done in sleep woodenly with arms,
slow-stumble-flight, making a moment
disproportionate, ten feet over the creek,
this presence I want to run after, but don't,
seen now and once before.

Up the hill planting trees,
one dogwood, two flowering peach,
kneeling in the cool Easter dirt,

on the last one, devotional and vain,
why turn and look,
I don't know, but here's the biggest bird
I've ever seen, huge, bluish-grey,
stretching between hemlock and laurel,
moving slow against the creekwind,
legs and body hanging almost straight down.

Wait, says this presence I'd forgotten could exist,
*wait. Don't stay up late
imagining, neither awake not asleep.
Be exhausted,* lifting
off the balcony in a backdive.

Jim Kilgo says what I saw was a Great Blue, a heron,
not a crane, "though people call it a crane."

The first crane I saw when I was seven
with Lucian by the lake, the black man
who worked at the barn and lived there
above the tack room, he with his shotgun at sunset.
Two glowing cranes
flying high and west, no struggle or wobbling
at that height. Maybe he didn't think
shotgun pellets could reach that far. Idle,
curious aiming. Blam. A long moment.
The following crane folded and dove
like a starving pelican and sank so
when Lucian rowed out there was nothing.

That was summer 1945.
Two atom bombs. Nobody knew
what they were. Now with cranes
so rare, I'd push the gun
off toward empty air,
if I were quick enough.

I want to purify myself with constant love,

till the vision of a sixfoot beanpole crane
stretched over the creek

be just a sight I have at five-fifteen, March 23rd,

with praise for being awake, for sleep,
for memories from both coming clear,
as happens,
when I'm not afraid of being, being
the gooney, flying bird's head with long spoonbody,
or the other I see in the carwindow's reflection
with vague eyes full of fear
It's a look encouraged here,
not likely to be shot,
unless it let go and rise
from the wading pool
in a new knowing.

Coley and I once talked to a screech owl
that flew in and down the stairwell,
and lit, swear to God, on the top rim
of Coley's big picture he drew of an owl.
When I held up Coley's left crutch,
(a broken leg bike-jumping off a ramp)
the owl stepped on to the end
and glared fire riding the crutch
to the door. Fear and rage distilled,
clamped in place in that small body.

Owl turns to the night behind him, turns back
to us standing on the doorsill, then the weight
on the end of the crutch leaves,
four wingbeats and a long slide
through trees. That's what it's like
to be healed.
These birds are pictures of our being alone,
at large: light flight,
then back to a fearful perch.

We are such fluttering monsters
moving within several shapes, till some appearance
surprises: A new love
puts her head to my chest

and listens.

Later a call
from that direction, Yhhhhhhhuuuuuuuuu

Fear.

In the Woods, You and I

Years inside a sleep, the woods
melt to an edge of trees, speech
trails off in a field, my child
forgets what he wants.

You reappear and stand beside a house.
You ask to trade places.

I shall be the written words and you walk out
among this other.

You whisper into me, *You've made love to just about everyone
there is. Now it will be me doing that.*

I understand, I become these long writings.

I believe in things that were strange before:
the tangle of figures in Malaysian art, something waiting
inside the haloed heads of Flemish paintings. No gold
around his baldness at all, the patron kneels
with his hat in front of him on the ground.

The current where it dips around a rock
has strands of light inside it.

The fields are covered with forest again.
My dreams come back more clearly.

That we recognize each other
is the finest act there is,
naked and nervous in these small white diagnosis rooms.

This is the true condition of middle age.

We pick our way through the brush, lifting branches
with whole cities lightly attached, that falling,
are not cities at all.

Fried Green Tomato Sandwiches

They may not go back to their marriages.
Tonight they're frying
slices of green tomato in the dorm room.
They don't know what's going to happen.
I'm just passing through this six-week
summer program for honor students,
two days and I'm gone. These two
new lovers are teachers for the whole
month and a half, with two weeks to go.

They're finicky about the heat on the electric frying pan.
She slices the green tomato toward her with the paring knife.
He does the flipflop of the flouring.
I put a thin layer of mayonnaise on the whole wheat
and arrange the lettuce leaves,
happy enough not to have love problems.
I love them both.

Let green tomatoes stand for innocence.
The frying pan for how much they want this love they have
now, longer. Though everything stands for that,
to them. Then who am I over here
with my knife in the mayo,
hungry as anybody else? No woman
fixes supper with me
regularly. May be
I should worry more about that
than I do. She's here, I tell myself,
but unseen, unmet, as yet.

I'm no priestly bachelor, for God's sake.
Though I do honor the calm, sweet light

around these two, I don't long to be
in love again, their kind, but I do
long for love to fill me. I can't explain
what kind. I help them fix and eat
their strange green sandwiches
and feel like I can wait
less restlessly now
that I've been here with them,
doing this.

A Walk in the Botanical Gardens

We get it in our heads
to inspect the undersides of each
waist-high Queen Anne's lace,
to find the black bug always at home
in his apartment of green scaffolding.

I don't understand why we want each other so much.
Some of my wanting is curiosity.
Each time, here's someone living inside.
I want you. I want you.
What are we saying.

Eventually we eat the flower of our need,
bug and all,
and we're just out walking nowhere,
with no schemes.

Bedclothes

She whimpers in her sleep,
when I move in half-sleep, quarter,
makes with me, for me, small, consoling, fearful
sounds, *urrhhh, unnnnrrhhh,* as a mother cat
talks to blind kittens, comforting and warning,

afraid they're about to get up and leave.

We go on tossing, talking to each other,
not conscious. I see it
in the robes and draperies,
folds of sheets and covers so in need
and moving, white edges of waves,
bedless, houseless bedclothes
with naked lovers, swaying
exhaustion, ocean kelp.

And the same robes and draping
frame mystical paintings, clothing
scenes of God's Presence—Gethsemane,
twelve-year-old Jesus with the elders, Jerome
in the wilderness, da Vinci and Dali,
Winged Victory and damsels from Rubens, tangled
in the same cloth, definite folding
edge, and changing.

Answer something to her grieving desire,
falling back into comfort and no-comfort.

We're waiting till it's over,
this strange energy-ocean.

It's a chief mystery to me
how we last as long as we do,
seventy, eighty years.

There must be some tender, possible, other-place,
composed of land, a tree, shade,
a bench with an old man talking about death,
maybe even the moment of death,
both of us taking sips of tea
the color of air with the sun going down.

Is this an old nostalgia, to sit
with whoever we call Philosopher, father, him
and his quizzical questions: Whether things are different
or the same, whether I believe the thing I deny,
what we both can know. I want to hear

his tone in this conversation.

Instead, we're walking through an open basement,
nothing left but brick piers. Between them,
mounds of thick shards of glass, jade,
ruby, bright orange-yellow. We call it
the glass factory, my brother and I.
It looks like an abandoned industry. Who knows.

Sacred and unexplained, dangerous to the fingers,
it's not a place I can believe the image
of bedcovers and luminous paintings
all being the same. That doesn't seem true now,
even such a short time afterward,

though the wanting to sit on a bench
and talk calm and honest
with an old man
remains.

We Have Written Out Our Dreams

We have written out our dreams
and brought them hear to read. The man
walks back and forth across a stage
with a thick arrow in one hand like a roadsign.

When he points it at any one of us,
as the signal to begin, we can't.
We barely make a noise, a highpitched
helium sound. He starts his tricks.
He points again. The clothes
of one woman sail across the room
to land in place on a man.

No unzipping or unbuttoning,
the man's pants and shirt and underwear
slide off over his head through the air
onto her, another perfect fit.

Titty-Bream

Some days it seems like a spontaneous play.
All I have to do is nod and laugh and watch
what comes next, with great interest.
The waitress approaching for a coffee refill,
"Now you're going to learn what
                                    fear is."

And here's John Hillenbrand, trying to convince me
to go fishing with him, describing a bream
that's too big to hold in one hand to get the hook
out. "You have to press it to your shirt
to keep it still, working
                            the barb loose,

that's a *titty-bream*." With us, listening,
is Lisa, of the most beautiful breasts I've seen,
ever. They curve like wide banana boats. They are
wise. The adrenalin is noticeably revving
in our fish stories. In the parking
                                    lot later,

she says the stars are more out, out
in the country where she lives. One night
they found Saturn accidentally. *The rings
were clear, and two of the moons.* "Please call,
if you get that in your lens again,
                                    Lisa."

I've always wanted to look deeply into a glass
tunnel and see Saturn at the far end.
But I wait too well for the near as well
as the far. I haven't the presence
to say, "I would love to undress you.
                                    Let's go

to the starlit country." Naaoooooowww. Soul,
dear face and breasts of Lisa, whatever I want so
much, the carwind late-at-night, no one on the road,
light in the eyes and on the water, secret light

inside a telescope, my passions,
                              don't be afraid.

Sleek and near, I lift you and whisper
in your mouth how I love the deep coldness
that made you and holds you with Saturn,
warm against cool, our favorite nakedness,
feeling the live bream
                    against my chest.

Summer Food

Green, the shape of a man,
with the insides of a woman,

they swim and dive around each other
in the boiling water, like porpoises.

O, to put the whole pod
of okra in the mouth.

Tomatoes, it is time to taste
ourselves, in these wet, red rooms,
the rooms of our mouths,
where lives the sigh
of language.

Corn, the tassels pull apart,
ears and silk, ears and silk and teeth,

Cantaloupe, a globe in tight webbing,
crisscross imprint. The onion underground,
in crumbs of dirt and old fabric.
Heat waves take form. Without panic or fear,
the air becomes visible.

Cucumbers, turning and sinking in the vinegar bowl.
I hold a head of cauliflower in my hand.

It's the head of someone whose name escapes,
which is not so strange. There are many names

for the ones we love, and wonderful to say:

Broccoli, Lettuce, Cabbage,
String Beans, Snow Peas, Pear,
Watermelon, Pomegranate, Plum.

Let us eat the solid forms of sunlight,
and walk around after supper
in the gold time,
loving each other and talking vegetables.

Kindling

This woman I am with
is having her palm read
by my friend. I'm not allowed
near. I go off up the hill to gather
kindling in the apple basket. Cracking small limbs
from the brush, I see them down on the deck,
laughing, faces close, hands
mending together.

Here with the sticks,
I find something, a numeral,
a wooden number one, streaked and flaky red,
with a rusted chain attached. I carry it
back with the full basket, hang it
over the fireplace, and wait
for praise.

Forty-five and sour with jealousy,
I wish this would pass,
and I would give up,
like these dry water-throats,
to being just a friendly,
apple-munching fire.

The Fire

The flame in the fireplace is the hair
of this room, of our being,
the going and staying waterfall
I light to watch fall up.

There's no sharp division between flame
and its light. Fire loosens
in the cells of the log a closed hotel
of rooms, loosens wood like string,
unties water, pssssswwwwwwwww,
opens the dead xylum.

It runs along beside me, it walks, it runs,
it has strong feelings about everything.

And no edge defining it
from its light.

The Wind Today

A slight pressure of Spring air.
We hold our breaths together
to stop your hiccups.

Listen to the machines, the sound of my salary:
coffee-maker, washing machine, stove-eye
boiling, and here the car comes back.

I'll tell you, since you can't see inside here,
reader, we're fixing supper,
we're drinking red wine on the stoop,
and eating corn on the cob
as it gets done.

I imagine the demons will find us again,
as they did last night.
Forgive me if you can. Today,

I'm the blind man
sticking his head out the window.

Orange Circles on Lavender Wings

A moral question for the intuition: How *long*
to keep coming out by this pond in Oconee County,
hoping the dog will show up, the dog
my son lost track of here unbelieveably,
she's such a whiney crybaby wanting total
attention and constant contact, and what
he was doing anyway with his friend Jim and Jim's dog
on Jim's father, Rufus' many hundreds of acres, remains
mostly unanswered. This is my fifth time out twenty miles,
walking this kudzu-engulfed-and-lizarded road
to hear App bark just once. All the way in to the slime pond
with the rotten dock, up through pines past
a deer stand to a scrawny orchard
with my whistling and calling, baffled
that a runt of the litter, five-year-old, spayed collie
could be lost in this tangle, or ever leave the safety
of road for any reason. I try to grieve
for my dead dog, and my cold, quick son,
who seems so little concerned, and uncatchable
in his escape cars. I haven't cried yet
over the dog, gone four nights, probably
lying down eaten up with ticks and mosquitoes and hornets,
or shot by someone for a fox, or maybe alive,
decided to go wild, unlikeliest
chance. This long.
Tonight's the last after-supper run.
Then I'll put ads in the papers, and it's up to how
it is to be. In my mind now she seems a little, loose,
leathery pod, like those hanging on a bush
outside my cabin, and I'm not there so I can't check
whether this one's rotten inside, or broken open
with whatever it is free and flying around with

orange circles on its lavender wings,
close to my face.

**

Second stanza.
The girl down the street whom I've called
"sentimental doglady" goes out, two and a half weeks after,
knocks on every door of a housing development,
locates word of a thin, tick-crusted
something, wandering the area, stays and waits
with her husband, and there's the dog!
By God, I change my tune
about crying and giving up hope.

Let the Door Be Locked

We are driving back from Hamlet at the Anniston,
Alabama, Shakespeare Theatre, going to a cabin
on Weiss Lake near the Georgia line. It's after twelve.
A green Camaro comes past the other way and does
a sliding one-eighty turnaround in a dirt road
intersection. I see it in the rearview
and speed up, suspecting some playful, country
viciousness, the kids excited like it's a movie.

The Camaro stays inches off my back bumper, no matter
I'm going eighty-five or fifteen. He doesn't leave.
I make a big loop-circle through a closed service station,
he's there all the way. He even pulls off the road and stops
with me, three inches behind. It's the strangeness
of not being able to see his eyes to gauge
how demented. This is not a movie.
It's such a shadow-whitened full moon night,
he cuts his lights to disappear for a second, then
reappear as a dark bulk speeding in place.
He *doesn't* pull in the driveway.

The following afternoon in the parking lot

at Desoto Falls, here's the Camaro with a guy leaning
on the front fender. *Would you like a beer?* Sure.
He goes back to open the trunk to fetch it,
I guess, from a cooler. "No thanks, that's
all right." I can't see walking over and him handing
me a beer, if that's what it was to be.

Whoever finally catches up with me and says pay
for all incompletely-lived, held-back-on
moments will be some innocent stock-car fan
with no idea what he'll do next.

I love to see it and talk about it, Shakespeare's truth,
but I've never said Hamlet's lines that change him,
those with the practice tip off the sword.

Any number of vague, driven moments might be out looking
for me now, some one of my random crazinesses
I could let stand for comeuppance. Shakespeare
has ways to open the curtain wider, out-loud attitudes
toward having run out of choices in front of a bunch
of people. I don't know what to say next till I am
what I know now, and that not constantly enough,
so my talking's about half-believeable.

Hymenoptera

It's clinically wrong, but this begins with a drink,
alone, back from the Emergency Room, cortisone
in each hip, welts heating up in clusters
on right arm, chest, back, inside right thigh, left
shoulder, and between the eyelid and eyebrow,
twenty-one stings. I'm not sure
yellow jacket or hornet. Doctor says it doesn't matter,
both hymenoptera, *Little mean bastards,*
they go for the eyes.

A wonder of innocent membranous wings again
after six years, come to me not wandering, but in

my own remote meadow-yard, swingblading
what I take to be my duty of tall weeds. Now
days of itchy skinconsciousness, thankful
to be anywhere, burning to scratch blood. They smell me
with my venomous sensitivity, me especially.

I have heard what some objective someone said: *Coleman
is riddled with fears*. Well that may be,
and the problem then: to boil what mixture I have
into soup, a glad courage to be sipped as I walk
back without a shirt to retrieve the swingblade
where it fell, skin so awake to air
and any slight furry hair of bee that lights,
forerunner, pre-bee of swarm-to-come
that can't be fended off, the thought of which
mustn't. Last night this dream. A woman
lines up juice glasses, drinks for me, clear liquid.
In the bottom of each, under ice cubes, is a live,
moving-its-legs, bee. I'm expected to drink
the stingers down. I'm hesitating.

I didn't see what I hit in the grass that caused this.
Often it's clearer. I've known when I was swinging
into a hive-nest and gone on slow-motion
with a long swing. Make-happen and let-happen,
and other happens out of nowhere. I can't untangle
the green wire, but I know the feel of that sound
around my head. Swollen, blackening, and finally
patient, it gives me new eyes to see the lovely
obstructions, the bamboo scaffolding.

The air only seemed to be thickening into knots
that kill. I didn't foreknow these beestings.
I had the dream, but no clarity, the way now
I have angry bee-acid in me swelling
to circulate. Look at this line of drinks,
a future of juice glasses, each with a scarab
waking more and more in the melting
and the hesitation.

These are fearful gifts that I accept,
and cautiously hold to the light, and swallow,
biestings, the old word for the first milk,
which is clear, from the mother's breast.

Now you'll be crazy over bees, says Benjamin, Long Distance,
among my other fears of motorcycles, power tools, snakes
on low-hanging branches, and I summon them all
to let them hum around my head, one at a time.
I don't need another black hood of buzzing.
More than three, I hit the water quick,
and you can laugh if you want to.
I choose to watch my daylight panic as a rock does,
secretly covered-uncovered in the stream.

Some Orange Juice

An old drunk, probably about the age I am now,
broke in our house before I was born, broke in
my brother Herb's room. Herb was small and sick
with a fever and not at all frightened
by the stranger standing there.
                              "Would you like
some orange juice?" He held out the glass of it
he had on the bedside table. Then Dad appeared
with a baseball bat and led the man off, whose
name escapes. No one was hit, or prosecuted.

All that resulted from that bemuddled night was
that twisted-iron bars as though for a castle
were fastened on all our bedroom windows,
and I grew up looking out through those bars
at the river, and climbing on them.

I know more now of the blank confusion he felt,
the drunk, and I've done unconscious things too
that have had consequences like the way he affected
my view of the outside for years, who wasn't even

born then, and who has just as blind a notion
of what bad or good could come of some wandering,
dumb thought to go and do I don't quite know
what.
      Could I offer you some orange juice?

WRFC

My forty-nine entries
to the Name the Call Letters Contest
won me seventeen albums, but not the movie camera.

Under various names: Xenia Zed, Mrs. Jarvis Helms,
Lothar Tresp, Matthew Barrick,
through two contest weeks, carrying a pack
of blank postcards, mailing them
from different bars around Athens: The Chameleon,
The Frogpond Lounge, The Last Resort,
Friends, finding anagrams
in drunktalk, winsome,
raunchy, four-letter conundrums:

WIND REALLY FONDLES COWS
WENCHES ROAR FOR CHASTITY
WRITHING RARELY FEELS COMFORTABLE
WHAT REACHES FROM CHINA

Thomas Wolfe made lists
of what he had to eat, who he slept with,
towns and cities, menus, casual sex.
The *I Ching* says there's nothing wrong
with casual sex. A girl I met in a bar
in Norfolk threw the coins to ask.

WHICH ROOM'S FOR CHEATING
WHO RUNS FOR CHEESE
WIMPS RUN FOR CONGRESS
WEAR RATTY FUR COATS
WITH REVERENCE FOR CUCUMBERS

WE'RE RUNTS FROM CAMILLA

You see people walking by the ocean picking up shells
and shark's teeth to put in a dish on top
of the counter in the kitchen.

WIDE RUNGS FEEL CONFUSED
WHIPPING RUINS FAT CHILDREN
WALLY'S RICH FINGER CREAM
WILD RHINOS FLATTEN CABBAGES
WHARF RATS FORGET CHRISTMAS

There's no end to that either, the only sound,
the sound of their bare feet in sand.

WHICH RAT FEELS CUTE
WILL ROGERS FAILED CHILDBIRTH
WARTS REVEAL FEMININE CHARACTER

I keep saying friends I've never met
are looking for me. With the ocean
on one side and buildings on the other
they come up behind. In my dream
they say, *None of it's clear.*
All of it's drunk.

We consciously don't judge
how far down the beach we've walked,
or why.

WITHOUT REASON FISH CHANGE
WE RADIATE FLIRTATIOUS CHARM
WOPSIDED RED FOLDING CHAIRS

This wandering the bars to find initials
willing enough to be a sentence
is throwing one collected handful
after another, a writing class from years ago,
people you run into, any random
assemblage, back
where they came from.

And each of us gets an award for doing so,

a tiny leather mail pouch, worn
on the left breast.

Walk Soup

Arrive in the woods a late October afternoon,
put on the stove a big aluminum pot,
half-full of water. Empty in the green peas
from their plastic sacks kept safe from mice,
with the rice, in the ironlidded skillet.

Walk upstream along the stream-path the real estate agents
haven't kept clear, lots of deadwood for starter.
discover a strange sinkhole cave-place,
lizards living in and out the mouth, and something
bigger, the grass pushed down, a sliding-path.
Ferns brown now even before first freeze.

Walk back dragging long dead limbs. Scrape and wash
and chop six carrots for the mush. Soup on medium low,
walk the other way, with the creek, into the double spring
covered with waxy galax leaves, now getting on ground-foggy
dusk. A small dead tree needs pushing to break itself
and be guided down between its live kin and snaked home
through the rhododendron tunnel. Two rifle shots.

Meaningless tourist practice, puncturing beer cans
thrown to the far shore. Maybe some sweetnatured soul
yells from her kitchen, *Don't disturb the wilderness*
with that damn sniper-fire! They blessedly quit,
and here comes the scared big blue, low on the water.
Speak of blessings. Bow to the breathing flight,
wings go in, the body lifts breathing out.
Glide, and shudder when you read
of Lilith in her bird-form, screech-owl
sister to this, the day's grey-blue watery closing,
she the night-talons.

Can the need to be torn apart be soberly said?

Return to the soup. Slice green peppers,
undress and chop garlic. Undress onions.
Daub of butter shrinking in a skillet blacker
than any sky will ever be getting. Sauté.
Add these to these. More water, more curry, more
pepper. One more leg to the walk before full dark,
up iron steps along the road where powerline people
have been chainsawing, power I cook with
this minute. Here's a little pine tree
they left. Drag it back like Christmas.

Five whiting filets, cut in five pieces each.
Add a can of chicken broth, more curry, turmeric,
oregano, mucho filé. Put the top
on the al-u-min-i-mum. Add to all week,
the dearly loved heating-up-a-late-afternoon-
walk-soup-ceremony.

You with your soup spoon already in hand,
sit. Wait thirty minutes. Read. Be split open
for this we live. Is that the tearing needed?

Add this. One exhaustion knot
of wanting a woman off God-knows,
slow untangling of innards.

Is any man ready to marry Lilith?
Body's demanding beauty, Adam's first wife,
sexually willful, *I saw four guys today
that I would love to fuck.*

Who is here to marry that panic?
Put her raveling tendril-wandering
in your devotion soup. Turn off the stove.
Simmer clove and cinnamon stick
on a starlit walk in the icy creek,
nevermind your feet.

The moon comes up through the deeps
of water at your ankles, a smear of light
on the back of a stone.

And a barely visible night-bird swims away
in a sky that is nothing like soup,
free as fireplace smoke,
no patient stirring around an axis of heat.

The Premise

I can wonder who tends me,
and what this grief is grieving for.

The whole family speaking the suddenly-thought-of name
for the new sailboat, *Serendipity*! A week at the lake.
Over the top of a rise a station wagon
                              has backed across the two-lane
and stalled
                    trying to turn around quickly.
Sixty miles an hour, all tightly in seatbelts.
Shotgun, I'm the only one injured, face split open
against the dash, nose, cheek,
                                    temple bones obliterated.
Be quick and get it over with.
Very little jaw and teeth remain,
                              eyes hanging
on bungy cords over the abyss. Some hair indicates *up*
to the doctors. Existing mostly in their eyes,
in the mirror above the operating table,
                                    voices round.

I have no voice. Tracheotomy. One optic nerve severed,
the good eye swollen shut for months. Two Teflon orbits,
a Teflon forehead, twelve surgical hours just to rebuild
a tear duct. Wires and steel buttons to stretch new
facial skin across.
                    I wake up inside one operation,
in the white of a fire, my face
the hottest part at the center.
                              I spell pain
on someone's palm with a forefinger.

into a hole behind likeness,
a balloon, or system of balloons,
that I crawl through,   one   another,

                             another,
traveling with helpers, a group I belong to
called The Community of Friends. We want to live
in ways they won't let us.

                    "Crazy radicals."

Candle drippings melt
into a blank, call it inwardness,
after collision: what is, who am I,
should I be,

                    inside this iron egg?

Surgeons stare at bad snapshots from years back.
I don't care how I look.

                    I am wind,
and a tent
          floating out over water.

Defend me from rational insurance forms.

A masculine mask dug up and kept
in a museum: the flat gold face of Agamemnon.
He is a toy for this olive-gold looker
eerily here-not-here on the glass case.

His scissored eye-bites,
                    my milky openings.
His thin, hammered mask of character, finesse,
my cedary lair of breeze and silence.

Voicebox to eardrum.

                    Come in.

Voices from the grate near the ceiling:
"Do you think we're real?"

                    "What do you *believe*?"

"Why did you tear off your clothes and all the tubes?"

To say something honest,
all I want to do, ever again.

The breathing crew is here. "Eleanor."
Yes.
        "We are here to celebrate
your breath." I'm   flattered.

Could you get this conveyance   back
to my hospital room?
                "This is the plan: to have
twenty-five parties, all different. By the twenty-fifth
it will be Christmas,
                and you will be well."

Dear God, give me voice to say
I know they love me, but I need rest.
I cannot keep going to these parties.
                There's daddy taking pictures.
People beside the avenue have pushbrooms
to clean up the glass,
                noise thrown out.
I am the heroine.
            Ropes dangle down the windows.
"You must not breathe."

"Eleanor."
        "Hold your breath till you pass out."

There's a metal superstructure outside the balloon.
I don't have time to explain.
"Begin the dodge movements."
                "You are SO lucky!"

Constantly it happens,
the incomprehensible bowing into steel,
the somersault in like a mirror twisting,
no balance, no words.
                I am music
in a bed suspended between states, overlapping,

overreaching chorale, Bach voices mixing
with *Wondrous Love.*

Give me a single, practical

voice to go along with this
open-to-the-sky

thingamabob.

I have always thought I might become a holy person,
     prophetic channel,
so here I lie,

in weird, metaphysical solitary, holding
a long, cool, brass cross

tied to my bed railing. Forgive me, whoever changes,
nurses, hears. Forgive what? *Bedpan.*

Bedpan lets me

bank through the wall treetop level over a park.
Forgive who?

A no-thing sits propped on pillows.

A seven-year-old boy walks in.

That's not my mother.

I'm not going back in there.

An elderly woman in a hat tells me to write
when I'm angry, or lonely, or *pulled through,*
strained through a tiny hole onto a Honda
cruising the wheatheads.

I bat them with a hand held out.

"Our time is up." But I know better.
"I can't read that.

You wrote on top of another message."

We float free of the hospital, the city smaller and smaller,
all of us going to a certain death, the air thinner.
Happy to be finished. Smiling spreads
through my entire body, every concern over.

We glide together into a huge emptiness,
a view, a tenderness.

In the wheelchair a burst of warm air

        hits. The smell of cut
Bermuda,   thick, sexual August.

"Honey, put your foot back more on the footrest."
Doctor Caine lifts the left lid slightly.

                                  Sun,
and his funny face with big, blackrimmed glasses,
talking light,
            "Looks good, lover."

What if I haven't come back to this humidity?
Become a presence with no edges:
                                  a damaged bulb
with little ideas catching a side-glimpse
in the hall mirror being ferried into its old house,
                        a falling tiny something

        breaking up on the hilarious void,
                        E-L-E-A-

Run-running naked into the night street, severed
from whoever's back in the house.

                            No one person
can catch my small perfect body, but many can.
Each doctor's face, a compact mirror
                            covering a closeup
of a hook-injured frog.

Voices in Intensive Care.
                        "Here comes our wreck!"
Are you okay?   I'll be okay.

I am bleeding quite a lot around my lips.
I do not want to moan. I hear the beautiful, whole
voices of my children telling the ambulance driver
how it happened,
                who we were.
I know the road so well
when the attendant says we are a few blocks
from the hospital, I already knew.

I am lifted up to a large table, blinding light.

Blood pressure, nurses running. Several men
leaning over sewing. I don't remember
          any pain, just
the thread lying across my hair, pulled
again and again across.
                    Deep in the fall
one evening those same doctors sat with me,
"If you hadn't had the hair on top of your head,
we wouldn't have been able to tell it was a human face.
Just a gaping,
               surrounded by blood and flesh.
The top part of your face had been torn off at the upper jaw.
We didn't know where to begin."

                    I'm cold.

                         "We'll get the wet things
off soon, but we want to check your vision."

                              Come on in,
the door's open.
               There is no transition I can see.
We were just singing and being silly, and now this.

Repaired edges emerge
                    covered with rebuilt tears.
Grieving stands in a room so long
                         some blood vessels
break in his eyes.

Stiffnecked, brokenkneed, nothing stays
in this much suffering.
                    It finally itself
slopes away like a mountain surface.
Small talk,
          a sip of potato soup.

The sound a screen door makes slamming in summer.

"Who is it?"

In the sleep state once I was angry in a motel room.
A lover and I trying to make love, but the motel maid
keeps knocking, cracking the door, wanting to clean.

We get dressed and give in. She empties a trashbasket,
straightens a chair, then starts to leave.
That's all you wanted!
                                    Rage rises,

then suddenly, isn't. Nothing's the same.

The flimsy box of air and time,
                                    gone.
                            We are swimming
in an ocean, diving long arcs down into dark green
and up in amber.
                    Whatever the terms for this layered life,
we are a vast swimming.

I would like to show you photographs
of how I look now, how we all once looked,
                                    how now.

We sit and turn together through a high school annual
of the world at present. How beautiful you are,
                                    naked.

How leapingly, strokingly, you move about
inside this breatheable medium, peacefulness, freedom.

We vacate the premise and face a new face.

Vacations don't always end in disaster.

Sewn up, and doing sewing ourselves,
with tiny thread-talk
                    and shiny needle-divings,
we begin to live in ways
                    they don't suspect.

                "Whoever it is, come on in here."

Fivepoints

There's always more than we can take in.

Marylil appears just as I'm ordering,
so we have breakfast together.
She tells me her lastnight's dream:

people are translucent,
a full, clear light pulsing in the chest,
and sparkly light elsewhere over the body an aura,
like glitter.

Confetti. We're in a river that curves around
into "the world" and back out,
and back in.

We're picking up stuff in the world and carrying it out
to the other place,
machines and tires and pieces of iron.

That's our job,
like astronauts on the moon loading up with rocks.

In the flowing river up to our necks,
we accidentally brush against each other sometimes,

and in the touch the glittery sparkles
flake off our arms and hands, wherever we touch,

and the strong, clear light gets exchanged,
merging in the two touchers.

Remember, in the background, in the back of everyone's mind,
a voice says, *Remember where you came from.*

She rubs the back of her forearm against the back of mine
across the booth. *Like that,* she laughs.
Now I have to get back to work.

Each Peach

Driving eleven hours from Athens to Norfolk to see you,
I turn off and buy a basket of peaches
at a roadside place,
sit it on the seat beside me,
and look through the whole bunch one at a time.
It's like reading:

patches of dark purple around the pole,
overlapping lights and darks, yellows and oranges,
mixing over the photographically dotted
globe. In my left hand,
this many versions of Jupiter.

Each peach has a seam,
as though it's been split open and sewn tighter,
no punctures on either side,
the perfect obstetric act. We imagine
what was taken out or put in. We bite
through the seam and try to think.

My mouth around and in you, my tongue
in the folds of the pit.
Don't leave your body. Stay here.
I start to cry, I'm waking up, I'm not,
but my head and my eyes feel
like they're crying.

This is the present I've brought you,
a basket full of planets, these fantasy women,
my overload of conceit.

Is it true, the myth, inside the pit
there's a hidden almond that's poison?
Is that the next tree, the next
face on the phone?

Two rockets leave for Jupiter this summer,
to fly close by, take eighty thousand pictures,
and spin off with new power, one to Saturn,

one to Uranus, both to Deep Space.

Sex has such a pull on me,
obviously, driving this far,
a two-way, equal and opposite,
pull: one out, speeding, the other
in, as the peach sweetly holds the pit,
and the pit holds tight to a secret bitterness.

Green Rocks

In the two lights,
of campfire and sun going down,
we are within these fallen trees
and green rocks, as though night had come
and taken both of us early,
and we were the pleasure of night,
here before it is actually dark.

The Problem

All one fall, if I stand in the door at nine-thirty,
the Big Dipper tilts
over the wooden table on the deck,
pouring itself, getting clearer,
totally upsidedown over the hemlock by two a.m.,
with everything so drunkenwet
I don't know what else to do.

I try to learn to wait to hear
singing within/beyond creeknoise,
something not watersound,
music not metaphor.

I have heard it. That's all I know.

The Tree

I'm taking a walk
on a cool, April morning through the cemetery
under the homemade archway gate.

The strength of the ants is pouring up
from under a slab, collapsing the edges
of a tireprint.

A singeing groundfire has been here.
Someone has lined up four seashells on one grave,
conch shells, saved from the ocean, placed
as if listening to the ground like the saying,
Keep an ear to the ground.

I empty one
by shaking and turning it to loosen the spiral
of dirt and sand.
I put my ear to its ear,
this valve for the ocean.

In the almost total quiet
I'm wandering between the dead
and the dreamed, listening to a shell.

A slowmotion rainstorm
out on the ocean at night
blends and spends itself.

One love is that restful mixing
of freshwater and saltwater,
the great transparencies
inside each other.

Another love is work
the same as ants do, busy in the roots
of a live tree.

It hurts to look at them,
eating the mind and the imagination,
always at it.

Put your hands in the empty places.
Feel the ants along your arms.

Do the way the Ecuadorians weave Panama hats,
without looking, their arms underwater.

What is it we make here with the ants?
In the subterranean wetness
and freshness?

New hats,
strong black hats,
composed of dirt and woven
with roothairs, a nesthat for each of us.

How is it so late? It's almost noon,
and I'm walking around in a daze.

Do you feel the ants along your arms?
People jealous and irritated with each other
for not giving enough time, people trying
to find something they want to do
this morning. Listen to yourself

saying, *Do what you feel like you have to.
I don't care.*

We're dizzy and sick
with such carelessness.

Once I was being chased
in a dream.

I hid in a woodshed,
where there was a mother goat.

They looked in.
I lay down and shut my eyes and sucked milk
from the goat's nipples.

The villains were so startled
they didn't recognize me.

I lay down and sucked milk

from a nipple.

I wish I did lie down like that
and get up without dropping a sip,
without missing a note or a leaf.

Last summer a man said to me,
You can't see it,
but there's a tree, long branches
reaching out.

The roots are in the ocean
of the mind. The tips are actual stars.

My children imagine how it might be
to swim in various substances:
think of motor oil.

Think of a swimming pool full of mercury.

Think of swimming in the milk
of a spirit tree: a cloud
where distance blends in the idea
of distance, light mixes with thinking
of light, burning, with love for the sun.

Graves, the singed pattern on the ground,
a seashell, the ants, air
in a moving tree.

Loud and soft voices lift and leave a room,
humming with themselves outdoors.

Two people with the lantern off
sit just a few feet apart, talking.
There's a slight wind.

Work

for Ed Hicks

Bits of white floating in tall briars,
one your father's hair-tuft on its way to the river.
You catch it in your hand, on, with your hand, the play
or recovering what hasn't any longer the work
of keeping a place, out in the pure open like smoke.

Ed tried to take care of his father, who would go to the door,
open it an inch and close it, open an inch and close,
do that twenty minutes. He'd escape and wander woods
and swamp at night. Ed at the funeral
took the shovel from the gravedigger, did
the covering work he saw as his,
as well as helping with mine:

felling a tree, six of us with separate functions:
my son and I on ropes to keep it off the house.
Ed at the base with a chainsaw where silence
at the end of a life, a new attention, rushes
through limbs to more work, ant work,
to keep everybody warm and philosophic, *with*
each other, tranced in handmatters.

Ed has a dream where the family had gotten together,
but his father wasn't there. Instead, fire-letters
were written across Ed's forehead, Who Loved the Fire.
Ed wrote that question, or statement, he tells me,
somewhere secretly on the chimney he's been building
with his neighbor Herman these last three months.
Ed on scaffolding, Herman at the mortor box:
Herman, I'm building this for my father.

Ed's father did love fire and the firewood work
leading to sitting close and tending, fire a reason
and a danger working in the eyes, what keeps us
with each other, and strange. Work: being each
in the group, as talking moves to raving, reverie,
to insight, singing. Dying snag to split red oak

perfume, to smoky snakeskin climbing the tar-inscribed
chimney. We lose it. The work is trusting
such changing, wondering what trust is.
Watch fire come back again to doing.

Timed doing. One day
more perfectly timed than others we wandered at 1941 map
trying to find a new trail: instead a frame house
up a non-existent deadend. Instead, the Reverend Woodrow
Hinsley, retired. Could we walk your land?

Trail up this way goes to a big double white oak.
There's a rock altar there where I pray.
You all are Christians, aren't you?

We sit on his bench and add two to the rock stack
of prayer, four feet by six by three. It is a cord
of thinking about what is the work anyway.
Strength and some ecstasy of being broken to pieces,
as walking clears the self and a fireplace works
to be empty. A father dies into a son's work.
Ed builds a chimney and *serves,*
the smoky word my father used
for what we might be doing.
Do you know the Issa poem:

> The radish-picker
> with his radish
> points the way.

You call from the road.
He doesn't quit work. He
uses his to indicate yours.

Audience

One of the family legends
in our little group of five,
Mama and Daddy and Herb and Betsy and me,

is Dad's laughing all one night
after a speech he gave to the Rotary Club.

Dad was Headmaster of a boys' preparatory school
for forty years and very serious
about the moral growth of the young,
but every now and then, at enormous intervals,
his trickster would erupt.

The subject was Education, of course,
and he'd come across a very subtle satire
of self-important holding-forth,
a deadly treatise that sounded like
it was about something, but wasn't.

It was, in fact, similar
to the Monday afternoon chapel talks
he gave. He knew that and figured
a little Polonian high sentence
would amuse his peers at Rotary.

But no one got it. They sat politely
through one gust of fustian after another,
like church members at some imaginary
picnic on the North Atlantic
holding their outrageous chapeaux.

And having gone so far, he had to bluff it
through, so as not to insult them,
and accept their heartfelt appreciation
for years of service and thoughtful
consideration of the issues.

He barely made it to the parking lot.
He hooted all the way home. We heard him
coming in, a noise somewhere between
the funniest joke and a howl
for his life spent mouthing maxims.

It was good, flat-on-your-back,
don't-nobody-have-a-clue, ocean-laughing
and ocean-weeping, and we tried to join him in it,

but nobody could.

He was hilariously alone
there in his bedroom, adrift
and at the mercy
of a profound audience
that kept swimming back by
in the wallpaper.

This

After a long time of not, I light a cigar I'm given
for a baby girl, and sit like my father used to sit

on the porch, late, in the dark, in underwear.
Mother had gone to bed. I would sit with him.

We didn't talk much, or whatever we said was
just part of being inside a summer night,

with its one orange focal point,
the breath-lit sun of his silence.

Spring Lizards

Where the filter of the hill
empties, I dig a miniature circular lake,
a foot across and a foot deep,
and leave to let it clear and come back,
to arrange creek rocks around the edge,
and leave to let that clear and come back
to fill a mason jar and a coffee carafe
with spring water.

I have never been so slaked
with the mystery of freshness.

And now I've left for two weeks and come back

to find tiny spring lizards
living in the well-place I dug,
little waterbaby salamanders
under the sweetness of galax
and rhododendron around the opening,
that leads up through reticulated rapids
and invisible passageways smooth with giving
the patience and hallucination
of groundwater into this mouth where
beings play in the clear
like tongues, like sounds that hide
so instantly, or pretend to hide.

Nothing can actually hide
its fear or its wiggly joy
in so transparent a pool.

The Grocery Store

I come out of Bell's with a sack of stuff.
Leaning from the back window of a car
in the nearly empty lot is a child,

a boy-liveliness that a parent
might sometimes not-take
into the grocery store.
I've never seen him before.
"Hey!"
          "Hey."
                    "Which car is yours?"

"That red truck over there."

"A man's been in it."
                    "Oh he has."
"A man's been in it!"
He's pointing.

I touch his fingertip

with my free-hand forefinger,
like the Sistine Daddy,

but rather the child
is power source here.

What do we want from any artist
more than that he change

the parked energy
to love-teasing?

With the help of what's missing,
to sail out a sentence
that opens the air.

The Restaurant Woman

As though it were a restaurant,
we'd sit and have ginger ale,
or coffee, in the study,
in the late afternoon.

Now this morning in an actual restaurant in Taos,
I hear from another room, *Precious Cargo!*
When the woman comes in, I ask,
                              "Did someone say,
Precious Cargo?"
                        "Yes. It's on a baby's t-shirt."
"My mother used to call that to me every time
I left in the car."

Now I'm starting off tomorrow
for the Himalayas, and hear the blessing.

The baby has blue script
across a clean chest
and the dark seed
of human eyes.

"She's been dead seventeen years."

"Sometimes they talk to us
like that."

I want to ask was it a Post Office stencil
back in the twenties, or a logo,
or a line from an old song,

but it seems impolite
to press for information
with the graciousness shown.

Soft Applause

I must not be a public person.
I'm getting worse at readings.
I'm not even in the room listening.
I've slipped out.

I feel more *public* sitting by this morning fire,
writing, then getting up and fixing coffee
and coming back to the chair. Now I'm public.
I'm all over the place.

But this other, I don't know,
with everyone sitting here
like a painting of angels.

Though sometimes I like it a *lot,* the attention,
because sometimes I have tremendously bleak nights
when I can't sleep. They began forty-five years ago
at my grandmother's in Rome, Georgia.
I was alone in a high-ceilinged,
downstairs bedroom with a loud clock-ticking.
Everyone else was upstairs sleeping,
and I was draining alive
into nowhere.

I got through that night and bought a cabin
with a stream right under it, so loud
you can't do anything *but* sleep.

And so when I'm away from north Georgia,
and because I've been public in this other way,
it's a comfort, and it helps me rest,
to hear some of this sort of wind-watery,
softly falling down sound
we call Public Love.

Spectacles

A dragonfly airshow takes place
above the creek, two hundred, threading
an axis more precisely than swifts
over a chimney, whatever they are eating,
if this be a feeding dance, invisible.
They weave a gyroscopic sock
like the Buddhist image of Reality
as a net with mirror beads for knots,
with here every junction a dragonfly's
faceted zoom lens, each full
of every other.

It's unlikely a natural event would only happen once,
as we seem to in our brief spectaculars.
A headless form breaks up before our eyes,
and in our eyes, like a dying, infinite,
yes, the identity of water.

Vigil Notes

I didn't stay up till the end with my mother
the night she died. And here's the shame
from another vigil I didn't make it completely
through, though shame is all wrong.

I told myself I'd go from seven p.m.
to seven a.m., tending a fire, to watch and listen,

and I didn't make it. Sometime after four,
propped up, looking at the fire, resting my eyes,
suddenly it was six. The sun not yet up.

I immediately sat straight and began reading
Ramana Maharshi, hoping for some sort of spiritual hit
by dawn, though knowing the shame for falling asleep
is the same as the satisfaction of keeping a vow.

I felt refreshed by those two hours of dreamless doze.
Refreshment is a large service the universe offers,
and gladly accepted.

I heard, toward the ragged end of my vigil, what I took
as a degrading sign of failure, the toilet
left running, unjiggled, upstairs, the tank
with a balky gasket that needs coaxing,
or it won't re-fill enough
to stop re-filling.

I once came back from two weeks away
to hear that desertedness
in an empty house.

But now some sweet exhaustion absorbs
the sound with more than forgiveness,
and hears in its continuous emptying
a faithful pouring-listening
that never sleeps.

Nightwork

Su-T'ung-po had a nightlong discussion
on impermanence
with Zen master Chao-chiao.
Dawn, he wrote:

> *The sound of the mountain stream*
> *is a long tongue.*
> *The colors of the mountains are those*

of the pure body itself.
During this night we've stayed up there were
eighty-four thousand lines of poetry
spoken in the watersound.

Here's my nightwork: no conversation,
read one article in the current *Georgia Review*,
two sentences added to a prose poem,
that's it. Fiddled with the fire, set
the electric blanket on *lo,*
near-sleep listening to the full creek,
bookprint and handwriting insect-tiny,
washing in with the voluminous night.

Tu Fu Rephrased, and Kittsu

A drizzling rain feeds the moss on the rocks
and slows down the mail.
Inside the mountain's cold afternoon shadow,
a black bull makes a lowing noise.
By the river a white gull
screams out how hungry.

Inlaid hairpins drop to the floor.
She's sitting by her loom, almost crying.
This will not come untangled,
all day staring at threads.

New Year's Day Nap

Fiesta Bowl on low.
My son lying here on the couch
on the "Dad" pillow he made for me
in the Seventh Grade. Now a sophomore
at Georgia Southern, driving back later today,
he sleeps with his white top hat over his face.

I'm a dancin' fool.

Twenty years ago, half the form
he sleeps within came out of nowhere
with a million micro-lemmings who all died but one
piercer of membrane, specially picked to start a brainmaking,
egg-drop soup, that stirred two sun and moon centers
for a new-painted sky in the tiniest
ballroom imaginable.

Now he's rousing, six feet long,
turning on his side. Now he's gone.

I sound low-key,
but this is the way I howl an old hymn
in the plaintive bass-drone,
a charm for accepting what happens,
and a stubborn question,

<pre>
            in the
      why   val-
Say   ley
                      of death should   weep
Or   I
    lone   the   derness
        in   wil-
                      rove?
</pre>

There's no one to worry about waking
with my singing. I have loved them,
those two boys, so well
that they've left.

We're after the fact now,
out in nowhere again.

We're I, and I am a line of music
wriggling along like water
wanting to be ocean.

>   *dars of Le-*
>   *ce-*   *ba-*   *bow*
> *The*   *non*   *at*   *feet,*
>   *his*
>   *with his*
> *The*   *is*   *fumed*
>   *air*   *per-*
>   *breath.*

Singing and talking,
one vibrates with the other.
Vapor-mist-going-up-this-way,
cloud-come-back-around-down.

The old FaSoLa singers
would not commit to words,
until they ran through the notes,
in broken lines of rain.

The reverse of me rocking my babies
to all verses of Samanthra,
or *David's Lamentation,*
who now in a shower somewhere
murmur tunes they have no lyrics for.

> La la   la
>   sol   sol
>   mi   mi   mi mi
>   do

I never took them to church,
or told them stories about David,
or Samuel, or Jesus,
but they move like fish,
or tadpole-radios in the mud,
flat on their backs on a roof,
or breezing by.

Maybe any motion is holy music,
not only theirs.

Remember how it went,

then forget.

Sliding, forget more.
Sliding air in the throat, this song
it seems so soon to quit,
any shred of unfinished existence,

La la la
        sol sol
                mi

that somehow
is unbelieveably over.

The growing
        of the
                corn

over and over.

Our watery bodies keep moving.

        Hands give.

        Eyes weep.

        Feet walk.

        Shoulders swim.

        The throat sings.

        The chest hopes.

        The genitals wait.

        And the thighs,

their small-stroke dancing work of balancing and lifting,
the thighs,
              slow-move
a big riverlike forgiveness
we can jump in,
I and my strong boys, now men.

Some songs don't ever get completely sung.

They're sung by the blood,
inside creeks and rocks and air,
in some cellular Beulah land,
the harmonizing water sings them.

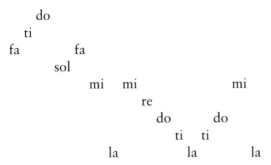

Darshan Singh and Christian Harmony

Friends have brought me
to this schoolhouse in downtown Santa Cruz,
no longer a school, but a meeting place.
Darshan Singh and Sawan Singh devotees
in one room, say the 2nd Grade classroom,
and directly across the hall, an ecology
organization, a real estate office, and down
at the end the Whosoeverwill Mt. Moriah
Baptist Church is using the old 4th Grade room
as their church this Sunday morning. Maybe
their building burned, or maybe they never had one,
I don't know. I'm down and across the wide,
worn, wooden-floor hall meditating
with seven Singh people.

When of a sudden, with no accompaniment, comes
the homesick sound of An Unclouded Day,
in the whinge and the whang
of a loudness I know.

O the Land of Starry Skies
Oooo the Land of an Unclouded Day

Ooooooo they tell me of a Land Far Across the Sea
Oooooooooooooooooooooooooooooooo they tell me
of an Unclouded Day

Floats me away. Do I want to be there or here?
Home, or home, or home, or home.

Where I'm from is some who I am.

As St. Augustine says, if what gets saved
is completely separate from my body, it's not me
that gets saved. Thence the doctrine
of the Resurrection of the Body.

My feeling is,

I can stay here subtle-Singhing,
or go to outloud, old-shoe singsong,
or buy some land, or save some wilderness.

It's all one fine, multi-purpose meetinghouse
and temporary sanctuary,
with a silverplated sugar dish
on a white satin pillowcase
folded for an altar.

I'll visit them all,
and walk the hall,
singing my half-quiet song
in a bundle of tongues.

> There are many rooms in
> this makeshift morning,

> And ways we've yet to let
> the schoolhouse be.

A Hard-Cuss for Gourd Seed

Out the sack and in the hand,
little dry nuthin' bird-turd,

him just lay here thinkin'
I'm a big fuckin' man.

You're a stupid rotten tooth.
Be like yo daddy, little
peter-in-the-wind. I spit
and thumb you in and hump

once to make you jump.
Bump up, jumpkin bumpkin,
you got this one sombitchin' chance
to be a gourd, or feed for ants.

Small Talk

For Mike Nicholson

Coffee

The oldest possible moon (left hand cups the waning),
transparent sphere about empty,
the experiment done,
in a dawn-blue so close, walking,
I keep checking my eyesight against a huge pine
rising next to those apartments.
Resolution clear.

Coffee at the Waffle House,
Suzie runs me off by calling in company,
"Sir, would you like to join this fellow in the corner?"
They're too busy for me to take up a booth
with my vision-notes. *I'm just leaving.*

On the way home on the topmost strut of the pine
is a crow, in the first actual seen sun,
an important spot.

awe-awe   awe

A messy, whacking, lift-off,
then a smooth-measured exit in a curving diagonal
over my intention,
and below the gorgeous
exhaustion.

My friend Mike Nicholson is dying
of an odd bone marrow cancer and kidney thing.
Just my age. As I pass his house, there's one lamp on
in the kitchen, figures moving. He and Tanna
making coffee. A bubbling moon one morning,
the next three absent.

This is one quick, bitter, steamed-up life.
We get shooed out before we're finished.
Fifty, I still don't know when's best to get up,
and when go to bed.

A spooked crow flies off in his animal sleep.
We walk to wake between various naps,
and one or two dyings.

I can't say what I feel.
I can't even feel it.

Mike is leaving early.
Is death better than being sick?

His eyes so wide and wondering, laugh so light.
"It's the medication, my friend,
chemical wisdom."

He's like a wonderful one-day Southern snow,
everything shut down. Everybody at home
on the phone.

Isn't it beautiful? It's so pretty.
I've been walking around in it.
Now I think I'll stay inside and read.
All the shenanigans I need
I can do from right in this chair.

The Second Mike Poem

I wrote your death-poem,
and you didn't die!

It was right moving too, but now here
like the last speaker of a lost Indian tongue
you stand in your shroud of invisible laughter.

The story is:
        You were sitting at lunch chewing
the bitter facts, how kidney transplants
in Sweden work in half the cases. Half live,
half die.
        And if you had a kidney handy,
you might chance it, like the mumblety-peg knife
off the left shoulder for the third time,
Chance the Game, rather than live out slow
dialysis diminishment.
                I can't stand the waiting room,
Coleman, those kids getting weaker every week.

Next to you, Rick Johnson says,
"You can have one of mine."
            And he meant it,
and the tissues matched and it's DONE.
Coin flipped, called, the new potato's
pumping, filtering, proteining-ing.
              By sweet damn,
you're here for a while-bit! A while-bit,
little piece of flesh. Bless the doctors, bless
the tissue-ologists, the analytic looks
down micro-tunnels, notes noted,
action: Cut, Sew, Mop,
             Laugh, Shake My Hand!

I don't understand what we are.
We're somewhat each other's fingers and voices
and eyes, as you are part-Rick now. Wave.
You-Who, match-mirror, through the glass.

We ride these flimsy bark canoes, talking
the upstream effort, and then the slide down,
poofing out air-sound at what seems a relief
within the overtone of an unseen drop-off,
getting louder, and funnier.

Where are we heading?
What are we saying
but a gladness
for being?

A knife stuck in the ground,
and the ground held. Not forever,
whoever said forever?
I said forever.

While you were getting cut upon in August,
I happened to turn to an Eliot poem. I never
read Eliot, except to teach him, and never this.
"A Cooking Egg." A stuffy, precious,
bad-laughter thing with these lines,

> "I shall not want Honour in Heaven
>   For I shall meet Sir Philip Sidney
> And have talk with Coriolanus
>   And other heroes of that kidney."

Don't you appreciate a literary reference
in your resurrection poem? Your happy-come-on-home,
flowers-in-all-your-pockets poem. Smile for me.
I love Rick Johnson. Here's your picture
from the paper.
                    Shitchyeah.
                    Mike, don't you like
walking around in a blue bathrobe with Sir Philip Sidney?
Ratty and royal blue.
                    Let's start a study group
at the Waffle House, and do the entire corpus
of S.P.Sidney,
                    and other heroes
                            of that KIDNEY.

We've got time.
                    I think they've lost my order.
                                        Who cares?
I can wait all day for my precious egg,
                        just looking at you again,
so skinny and cantankerous
                        and mean as a little bird.
I'm not even hungry.

Three

Now it's thrown back in our faces,
the acid of abscess and amyloid attack.

A month, and Rick's in an Atlanta clinic,
you're fading in Augusta.

I hear nothing but bad.
"It's been hell, buddy," you answer
the phone in Intensive Care.

They all tell us, the prophets,
that dying is like taking off a tight shoe
that you've worn all afternoon,
walking at the fairground.

Or much, much better. Flying inside music,
inside light. Snorkeling the indescribeable reef
of the soul, the myriad niches,
                            the pretty fitches.
You'll love it. I'll love it.

Let's get our signals right
before you roll over the side.

One pull is, *Hey, I'm here.*
Two is, *I love you all.*
Three is, *I'm loose and swimming
in the joy of God.*

Not that I have special information.
This is not so much belief as a big-time hope
they knew whereof they spoke, those old distributors
of these most delicious
                              loves and fishes.

Every Evening

I haven't done much with what's been given me
to do. I wander away and waste whole weeks.

Deathbed people scream, DON'T WAIT!
But I wait and waffle away
from clear warnings.

The cabin next door burns down
to a melted tire that could just as soon
be me. Mike may not make it
through Thanksgiving.

I love his fierce indignance.
Look at the damn wires.
We can hardly see the sunset.

He wrote a savage column last year
on mall architecture.
                    We haven't forgotten
what beauty is, but we've forgotten
to demand it!
                    And manning the Peace Booth
downtown: a smug young guy strolls up
with supposedly Christian slogans
for a bigger Pentagon.
                    Mike scrabbles
over the top like a bantamweight
going after the money changers.

To avoid suit, he had to endure a conference
in the fellow's pastor's polyester office.

Wonder he didn't chew the rug off the floor.
Wonder the minister's bookcase wasn't inscribed,

> *Mene, mene, mickle Michael Nichol-*
> *Son, I love your quick goodness*
> *fighting at my peace table.*

Don't wait to do what you feel here
to do. Obey the sudden truth.

Love the demanding beauty
of a bloodred late November sun.

Mike, let's crackle our imaginary walking
faster and brighter toward where that thing burns
inside its own and our sky-opened chest,
open to what death keeps beyond
us every evening.

The End of the Sentence

Home is where the art is,
without the he.

Home is where it's at,
without the her.

Alison is a painter and a carpenter,
and my love-in-the-making, and those are
our unmarried marriage-songs.

We live and love thirty miles and minutes
apart. Separate homes, same his and her heart.

Last night I stayed with her in Lexington.
We tried to think of the sentence
Mike put on the wall at one of his showings.

"It's difficult to write a *Paradiso*,
when . . . ." But we couldn't get the end.

"It's difficult to write a *Paradiso*,

when all the world wants is an epilogue."

Not bad, but not it. I drove back to Athens
this morning and went to look in on Mike.

He snoring away. Margot Rosenbaum is there.
"You writing much lately?"
                              "Well, yeah."
Mike opens his eyes.
                    "He's got a little telephone
by his bed that he listens to everybody's secrets on."

"I wish. Hey buddy, Alison and I were trying
to think of the end of your sentence,
'It's difficult to write a *Paradiso* . . .'"

When you're facing a conflagration.

"Right. We couldn't get it." He snores back,
days and nights reversed. The others leave,
and I sit there with the shades pulled.

The physical therapist slips in. "Do you think
he'll feel like some exercise later?"
                              "Gosh,
I don't know. Can he get up?"
                              "We lift him.
He went over to the window this morning."

I woke at Alison's,
staring into the drowningly open
day.
        A band of birds
                        shot across the pane,
and I felt how Mike
won't see that much detail again.

On his walker all concentration goes
to the exhaustion of one foot.
He tries to attack.
                    "I don't know what
any of this means."

"I don't either."
"Where's the fairness factor?"
"I don't know."
"Why do you keep coming up here?"
"I just like
to hang out. I don't know."

Outside in the air, I see a glory,
his searing, soaring honesty
lifting above my seed-picking.

I need to attack myself.

He is the hawk of human-ness
riding bright-cold winter.

I will never write anything else
about anybody's death,
and that's not what this is.

We don't die.
We just can't be
located quite.

The talk continues
on the secret phones.

Alison and I are so alone,
that we can love. We have to have
privacy, and we have to have
the phone.

It's hard to claim to be living in *Paradiso,*
when you're watching a friend burn
down to an intricate ember.

Mike winked at me out of near-coma,
and sang a faint, madeup song,

> Coming to the Station O
> Coming early to the Station

Alison said, *Sweet Darling.*

We do die.
Harp upon it.

We end.
We miss.

And the spirit's true too,
a tenderness stringing us painfully,
almost hilariously, out of these skeletal
identities like chimney threads
into one blind longing.

The Fucking Grave

These last twenty days I've stood by the tomb
of Saint John, by the lost grave of Luke, a hillside
to point at, by the supposed forearm of John the Baptist.
I've walked into the last house of Mary Mother of Jesus,
into the mausoleum of Jelaluddin Rumi, my sheikh.

I've shone myself in his brass candlesticks,
and nodded to tough Shams Tabrizi, who knows I'm not
ready to work on his book, and seen country-dawn,
hardworking Haji Bektas, with his hand
flailing some outrageous truth,
the closest kin to this,
                         God's saint ranting
in my chest, not out of a newly filled-in
nothing-hole in the Oconee Hill Cemetery.

Don't be absurd. Mike touches now the wide wing
of all being and art, and wonders what
the cawhompus comes next.

Now you're talking!
Finish wrapping.

I got home last night at four a.m. from Turkey,
gone there to see the dervishes turn.

At the Waffle House this noon
they tell me you died a week ago,
when as it happens, I was dreaming
that an old lover had died, and I had been
asked to find the right burial site.

I picked a place where she and I once
made love on the ground for the grave.

That was Mike in the spirit,
having fun with me, the *fucking*
grave, don't you see?

Help me finish this, friend.
Closure-clothes, to wind
it up, God bless it.

Kneeling and crying in the pantry,
wrapping Christmas presents,
I hear so close,
                    Finish taping the packages,
Coleman. The mail goes at six. Cry
for yourself. Your connection to God
could be much grander.
                    Grandeur!
The eighteeeeeen thousand universes!
Those sufi terms, what you been re-phrasing,
pal, they ain't but half-wrong!

                    (our laughter)

Is that what death is,
finally making love
in a way where gender
is fused asunder in some
surprise, switcheroo,
trainstation bed?

Whooooooooooooooooooo
        aunnnnnnnnnnnnnnnnnnnnnnnh
                Yooooooooooooooooooooooooooo

71

Salt

I hear me singing hymns,
full of fear and rosy pretending.

And this art and literature circus
is mostly preening and distraction.

I can crack Mike's whip a little,
since he's not here.

We need some salt
to get the truth more
grainy and bare.

**

We go out to buy our grown son a car,
a used one. We get down to look under it,
not knowing what we're looking for,
some burbling, viscous drip.

We're lying there on the ground in the car lot,
when we realize we can't get up,
without a lot of help.

That's a funny position to be in.
I do wonder how much of my "spirituality"
is fantasizing, though I would bet
this closeness *is*

a truth we come from
and thread back into,

like the freestanding waterfall
I saw once in a dream. (There's mystery
beyond betting in dreams.)

The waterfall flowed from the ground off a cliff's brow
and back underneath at its foot, visible
just in descending, standing
on its foamy nest, beginning and ending.

We are these pouring moments

of autumn water, as though a basin broke.

And there's no explaining
what gets stirred around
in the soup of our small talk.
We've just the taste.

***

Who's in that corner booth?
Some old ghost.
He must be an illusion.

I didn't see him much last year,
and this year's not any better.
He must be part of my very soul.

Look at that pigeon
looking at us. Makes me
feel like an aquarium.

***

Closed in,
to be stared at.

Endings want us to open out,
and not just trail off
the way I usually.

What I want
is like the woman I heard of
who dreamed a candle on her hospital
window ledge, down to its last.

The little wavering dance went out.
Immediately, her vision shifted
through the dark window
to an outdoor, skyscraper candle
lit with a strong flame.

Though it's not some huge vision,
not an image of anything.

I won't know what I want

till I quit thinking
saying it is it.

The talk gets even smaller,
closer to silence,
then is.

Ornamental Decisions

Where to sit in the sun
is the only true question,
when not going in to teach,
along with how not to feel paranoid
they'll find out and fire me.

Under pear-trees full-white nearly hiding
the red and blue university
postal kiosk, I choose
this bench and this new-heat
on my face, instead of talking
the history of my fear
thus far. Petal-sky overall.

I know who planted these, my friend
in the Law School, Milner's
wife, June. June and Mr. Forsyth's
forsythia, they bolster my floral resolve
to write letters in the sun and become
a man resembling an Asian flower opening,
with a curved knife in the center.

Or

We sit here trying to tell or sing
each other something truthful or tinged
with beauty or joy or some other empty,
full word that hasn't been ruined

by being overstamped, the die

blurred, before some fading thirst
we have or have had poisons us through
the water, or the very ground pulling through
good corn on the cob chomped on the back
stoop with sips of red wine, settles

enough bad micro-sediment somewhere,
the brain or the marrow, to make us
not any longer care, or recognize,
what in words or otherwise is
beautiful and/or true.

Becoming Milton

Milton, the airport driver, retired now
from trucking, who ferried me
from the Greenville-Spartanburg airport
to Athens last Sunday midnight to 2:30 a.m.,
tells me about his son Tom, just back
from the Gulf War. "He's at Fort Stewart
with the 102nd Mechanized, the first tank unit
over the line, not a shot fired at them.
His job was to check the Iraqi tanks
that the airstrikes hit, hundreds of them.
The boy had never even come up on a car accident
here at home, twenty-four years old. Can you
imagine what he lifted the lid to find?
Three helmets with heads in them staring
from the floor, and that's just one tank.
He has screaming flashbacks, can't talk about it
anymore. I just told him to be strong
and put it out of his mind. With time,
if you stay strong, those things'll go away.
Or they'd find a bunker, one of those holes
they hid in, and yell something in American,
and wait a minute, and then roll grenades in

and check it and find nineteen freshly killed guys,
some sixty, some fourteen, real thin.
They were just too scared to move.
He feels pretty bad about it, truthfully,
all this yellow ribbon celebrating.
It wasn't a war really. I mean, he says
it was just piles and piles of their bodies.
Some of his friends got sick, started vomiting,
and had to be walked back to the rear.
Looks like to me it could have been worked
some other way. My boy came through OK,
but he won't go back, I'll tell you that.
He's getting out as soon as he can.
First chance comes, he'll be in Greenville
selling cars, or fixing them. He's good at both.
Pretty good carpenter too, you know how I know?
He'll tear the whole thing out if it's not right
and start over. There's some that'll look
at a board that's not flush and say *shit,*
nail it, but he can't do that, Tom."

Fixing the Door

Fixing the bathroom door would require
taking it off and planing two sides
the floodwater has swollen so that
it will close only with a definite
effort and sometimes springs open
to reveal a sweetheart shitting
or myself to whoever's standing
by the refrigerator looking in the way
we will when we're not hungry for anything,
just checking as we do when any door
opens of its own volition. First,
I'd have to buy a plane.

Two-Hour Wait in Toronto

The sweet tone of our desiring
on the phone, Rachel, is I want us
to lie down and kiss, or breakfast
out in the sun at the restaurant
near the P.O. Do you feel
me feeling this?

Lana Turner, love goddess, whom I notice
here in the *Toronto Star,* is seventy.
Her first movie, a bit-part walk-on
in "A Star Is Born," 1937, came the year
I was born. Her story is mine.

We're discovered in the Top Hat maltshop
across from Hollywood High wearing this trademark
sweater, which we never took off, not for a one
of our seven husbands and a slough of real
and publicist-invented romancers.

No critic ever took her seriously.
This is also true of me.

Real-life drama came to Lana
when her teenage daughter, Cheryl,
stabbed to death Lana's hoodlum-lover,
Johnny Stompanato, who was threatening
to disfigure Lana. Cheryl was cleared
on grounds of justifiable homicide.

Maybe some violence threatened me too
in the early fifties, that I didn't understand
my role in, and can't recall repressing.

Then came 1957, and while Lana was Oscar-nominated
as the steamy mistress in "Peyton Place."
I am taken to bed by three TWA stewardesses
in the luckiest string of summer nights
ever threaded upon bare, forked being.

Is it repulsive, or funny, or just a marvel, how we

peak and moon around and change partners,
and wonder why we went where?

Nothing much since.
One season on "Falcon Crest."

Lana resides now on the twentieth floor
of a posh LA highrise with two large terraces
as exquisitely shaped as her breasts
used to be, turning their one hundred eighty
degrees from the desert to the Santa Monica pier.

It's her ivory tower, and since 1969
she has been quote "celibate by choice.
I am very close to God. I read the Daily Word,
and I have learned to meditate. The age-thing
is just a bunch of numbers." Unquote.
I couldn't agree more.

Rachel, I get smoothed and here,
with you coming toward me,
on phone or in flesh.

The plane is taking off this second.
You may not tolerate my silly-Lana.
So make me honest. I know another
beautiful Rachel, a Rajneesh sannyasin
who has written a very trying-for-truth book
called *The Orgasmic Mirror,* a journal
of spiritual feelings and sexual connections.

She and I are not lovers. Shall we
share erotic tanglings, you and I?
Who else but us will ever read this?
If the phrasing's good, many.

Would I trade what and who I want
for beautiful language that holds the desiring
and a little of its satisfaction?
Do I have to choose? Can't I have both?

How will men and women be more open in ten years?

Keep those predicates jiggling, camerado.
We're slanting into Cleveland.

I want to unwrap you, button by
button, by snap, by zipper. I want
to nurse your nipples. My desire wants
inside yours and then to change,
saying the shifts as we go.

I see Lana meditating
with a coffee maker drippling
nearby, her eyelids identical
to the Buddha on her vanity.

And now going out for a semi-reclusive lunch,
salmon sauce, spawning hunger spread over
her reaching into some table condiment.

In Cherokee the question is,
"How deep is your well?"
Not "How's it going?"
the car metaphor.

I want our native wellsprings mixing,
but I don't want to live together, or help
raise your little girl, though I love her.
I've raised two children, more or less,
but could we see each other more?

And I don't want to hurt your husband's feelings.
I don't want him to know. For God's sake,
these *I don't want's*. I don't want
to covet another man's wife, but I do.

Is there a way of wisdom wherein
there are no secrets, where these and those
won't matter? My noggin feel stroke-prone.

I'll tell you now a story that makes me crazy,
high over my country of origin.

My nephew Daniel became a fighter pilot,
because he didn't play football at the fiercely

footballed school we all went to, where
for three and a half months every year
from the seventh to the twelfth grade
we put on pads five days a week and blammed
each other in a galloping hormonal joy,
spent the aggression and the fear, did what
passed for heroics that didn't kill anybody,
and became great, relieved buddies.

Daniel didn't do that. He learned Tai Chi
and meditative calisthenics, so that
at twenty-six he hadn't gone through as much
careening bump-ass as needed, and had to
put himself through the scariest regimen
he could find, which was to land
Navy jets on carriers at night.

He did it the best of any in his class,
and then this Bush-Saddam madness arrived,
and he was sent, not as pilot, but as
a high-level liason with the Saudis.
He was right there in the Riyadh War Room,
and as January 15th approached, the old
commanders recognized that the quickest
gun they had was Daniel. They put
his lightning reactions up in an AWACS
and told him to direct the whole show.

When the Red Sea F-16's, when the far, land-based
B-52's, now the Brits, now the Stealth, and come on
you A-6's from the Gulf. For the first two weeks
of fighting he called our four-dimensional
square dance of death.

They sent him home early.
We had a family welcome dinner,
but he couldn't say anything yet,
where he'd been, what went on.
He hadn't been de-briefed.

He looked straight at me, "This war we do now

is not about making warriors." His laugh
was strange, and he drank a bunch
of martinis to no effect.

Whatever's-in-charge has damaged Daniel's
animal gladness, diminished his grief,
and given in exchange the Bronze Star.

What do I get? Dollar gas? Cat got
your tongue? I have a tongue-eating
Iraqi housepet I'm sitting.
Don't touch her.

Next to my phone is a list of culture sites
in Baghdad, which back in early January
I was going to write a magazine article on,
with color pictures, so we could see some
of what was there, before we destroyed it,
unlike Hanoi, which nobody knows what
it ever looked like, but I was way too slow.

The tomahawks were already lifting from their racks.

1. The Al-Gilani Mosque for Abdul Qadir Gilani,
my teacher's teacher's teacher's teacher.
I go that way back, and other ways too.

2. The mosque on the spot where al-Hallaj
Mansur was martyred in 922 A.D.
for saying, "I am the Truth."
Hallaj, godalmighty.

I won't continue naming the twelve jewels.
I'm too slow, but I know this
is a deep well, Rachel, where everything
dissolves into love-poem.

Feed me. I need your milk. Take off
your shirt. I need to suck skin
as if it weren't imaginary.

We're not seventy yet, or celibate.

Wantings change, and we begin
to see what's in them.
Which way now?

Lana's real name is something else,
we learn at the end.

Who am I? Am love and truth and confusion,
and a lost bear trying to walk along
with several angry sweethearts.

Don't fuck your life up because of me.
This cultural anger and eros dance
may not be one you feel led to join.

It's mostly a waiting. For what or whom,
I don't know. Rip Van Astronaut
sits atop his gantry twenty years
dreaming ignition. My psychoanalyzing of

Daniel and his humbly efficient pilot-buddies
may be more saying *I* am skipping exercise
that could calm this shadow-rage.

And/or it may be true that young men feel such pride
of mastery in their machines that they lose
compassion and cannot imagine anymore
the shredded organs their ordnance feeds on.

Never enough. Daniel will write his Iraqi memoir,
as Rachel her own account of love's fumbling.

Because writing is also waiting,
like this full of hurt laughter and wanting
a new double love-poem, meeting in the come-close,
come-close, then repair to separate balconies.

Because it's not you now, Rachel,
and it's not Iraq. Desire and anger
switch to quicken elsewhere in the months
or year I've fiddled with and forgotten,
this trying to get them down in language.

I tender words to see if after a while
they'll toughen to a shape.

No sexual trance's what waiting's for,
no being with another dying being.

Can it be it's not getting laid,
or living with a truelove?

There are things to do,
other than exchange juices.

My breathing bumbles and disrupts.
I'm not Lana. These next fifteen, secret years.
Give me a good quote, Miss Turner!

I want sexual excitement, but less and less.
I want my breath to stay deep and strong,
to feel some risky truth moving there.

Because beyond this poosh, and the back in,
a heard-shape of nightwater rushes by,
the emptying flume of mystery
that I've seen in one person, and is
what I long to have come flooding through,
so that the waiting will be less and more
a helpful hinging out into sun, or folding
into a room, however is needed for faces
gazing back, the being whose water
of presence washes around us.

Mistrust and lying, jealousy and some desire,
feel closed off. Live inside the listening
conversation that is our joy and art.

In what my new love from Toronto
says and does I hear the gift again.

Though we don't seem to want to be together
for more than a month at a time. We go
back and forth, splitting airfares.
We have no rules but to stay
conscious and honest.

Which is a lot, and we're not
very successful so far.

I'm fifty-five and've never tried this
with a woman. I'll hush. *Faithful*
and *unfaithful* are these ribbed cloud-racks,
so many soluble compositor trays
I descend through, this surrender afternoon.

Nothing to obey or disobey.
What I feel, who and if to live with,
are not known certainties for long.

I wait and act and say and write things
for the energy and dissolvings
love seems to require.

Wagtail

She and I, we're
walking downtown and see
a display that's not a display.

It's really happening, a woman
is being raped by a bear in a drugstore
window. No. It's not rape. She shivers
with delight and with slipping down and off
her stockings to enjoy the more
beneath the bear.

He lumbers to the back of the store
between the aisles of little bottles.
She stands, and pulls her great robe
around her, turns to the crowd,
confident, middleaged, calm.

Opens the cloth butterfly wings,
and hanging between her legs
are her sexual organs,
and her womb.

"Pretty gruesome, huh?" she comments,
and breathes in deeply, everything
going perfectly back in place.

You may not want to hear more.
You may not like me for telling this show.
I won't be led by applause, or none.

The demonstration's over. The crowd
moves away, mostly repulsed,
or not interested.

She and I will stay for this pair
to do what else they may,
and the waiting we stroll inside
is the unknown we came so suddenly on.

The drama done with a bear makes
a few companions only, those
that want the gruesome pretty.

I look that word up because of how
precise the choice, though wondering
why not *grisly*. It comes from *grow*,

Old English for trembling, the *grues*,
the frisson in a sprout, the palsy
of hand-to-hand.

Solemn bear, she breathe in, bare out,
in, butterfly breathing and bear pants,
seed in wet crumble. I take
your dancing hips in my hands
and enter the haunch-waggle.

"You'll like it back there," you say,
"And hold my breasts. They've gotten
so lovely for you, and me."

There and there. How much
will I admit that I pretend
to live in your mythology,
just to be friends with

our bodies' timidities?

A caterpillar secretes a chrysalis
and becomes green mush for the next,
which is our wings waving over
the deep flower of our unmade bed,
something lighting on a mirror.

I do not know the answer
to anything.

I am at your breast, a boy-baby,
who can miraculously talk and sip
like Shakespeare in a bib
with his wondering mom, and listening
to her day, which isn't enough.

Must we figure what
means what when
in the grip.

If it's angry and funny,
is there tenderness?

Like *suck* and *fuck* and *masturbate,*
which cannot be washed clean of anger
and shame. *Masturbate* comes from
"to rend oneself with one's own hand,"

which could, though, be like a seed husk
does to let the cotyledon up into light,

or the pod that ripped to let the velvet-robed,
brown-and-purple-ringed, wood nymph stand
in a Mason jar on top of my refrigerator.

English sex words are ugly. Though Whitman
lets the dawn put up libidinous prongs
and spurt seas of bright juice,
still he can't let his bear-
goddess' lust show much.

He's mostly in a smoothed out warmth

for the countryside, and the cityside,
and they that dwell therein.

To try and be more honest, sex does stretch
to include the public attitude, and sex stays
ludicrously rooted, and the two sometimes
turn over, lose connection, and laugh
a raw, imperfect wheeze that feeds
our insides. Sex is a gruesome
growing-heave, and fine
stitching too.

The bear humps the goddess,
and the goddess humps you.

But this bear and this woman
won't be where we found them before.

Walk around town. Enjoy the garden
in the growing season, the shock
of splayed nakedness. Rush in

to that, and the words, the uck, thuck,
ruck, cocky-duck, sweet-sticky
footprints on a mudflat,

about the only sounds we make for how
we pull and fold each other for one
face beneath the bedspread-mask.

"I cannot quit
biting your shoulder."

Wagtail, we're touched
in the heel.

Wagtail, these drumskin bodies give
building-motion to some huge music,
a sexics: the salt tongue-tip

of a wave riffling like a tambourine
in a courtship dance of whispering
around the rock-nipple caesura:

everything we speak and make and don't mention:
whatever consciousness is becomes ridiculous
energy-drips of wriggling balsam,
so aromatic with effort,

that even wronging Anglo-Saxon tastes good:
Fuck me, you say, and I frog back, *Right now.*

My secretly thrown-to-the-wind bear woman,
others I'm with I'm not who I am,
till then you come in any

room, field, or street,
and we stand and walk together
through the astonishment of seeing,
like a grassfire racing to its death.

Night Creek

Rain-listening sluice, well washer,
hurler of horse troughs against the roof,
waterbody rising unnameable over the meadow-slant
to burrow every secret storeroom of yellow jacket nest,
dissolve the Turkish mud-dauber caves under the joists,
fill the shallow pewter spoons of the horseshoe pits
with ringing silence, and for one moment film the deck,
soak the rug level with these insoles, unfooted
and footed, and through each eyelet caress
the skin arch of who sits alone reading,
with now no light, the unheard transformer blown,
to hum and slightly list-lift the house-bubble
three inches downstream, no more, certain warning
and smothered applause. The spices jostle watching
from their three aristocratic rack-balconies,
some wanting to flavor such a huge soup with paprika
and oregano, some to just stand unopened,
the cardamom, the anise seed, the dried rosemary,
for there will be no delicate enhancing of taste,

the while this confusion covers the first shelf,
smoothing the mystical spine of Gregory over
Niffari's visionary shreds and into Sanai's
gateless garden pool, the overflow-memories
immediately detaching from their fictions, where
this melted cup came from, why a one-button-eyed bear
sits with a snake-stick and an oddly triple-cracked
budvase, how this iron skillet followed innertubes
through the rapids one August afternoon, wobbling
its shoulders through the boulders, and would not
be sunk, foundering to some use now unrecalled,
like this broken-off stalagtite compacted of slow-tears,
and the second shelf with its Eskimo healing chants
and Taoist drinking songs, and my mother's college
English Romantic poetry anthology underlined
in red, and now my thighs suddenly peninsula
toward the third, a line of Russian novels
and the Macchu Picchu picture book. This is how
everywhere comes at once into being, sopping
bookprint to an unreadable paste,
with the bridge crossed quietly two miles downroad
plunging past so close, an enormous swimmer
made of telephone poles, flopping odd angles
to the flow, a monstrously drowning dumbshow
of what's not been loved enough, the failure seen,
and then there's peace in water-patches,
one of them circular, balanced around my collar bone
like an antique Dutch wedding costume,
that because I never put it on, returns for
a new rehearsal where furniture cuts loose,
and endtables romp to the door, and my mouth
fills with an unblinking, no-longer-thirsty rose
opening its silken hallway above my forehead,
the passion I swim within, a new creature
slipping through the dark water,
shaped like a normal breath, a trout-joy
exploring what begat and will re-absorb, a slim
alleilulia cruising the sunk fridge, and effortless
mandorla round the carpentry edges of the counter

like a worker's hand fiddling rearrangement,
a faint glow of decision, parting slightly
the sliding glass where morning begins
its earliest Spring flower pranks,
the turtle-streaked music of dawn, with these lips
a mere hole mouthing an invisible breast,
the lure of a flooded throat where the sun comes
nudging through a fine lawn of marine distinctions,
its face: am fish, am drowned man, am-am-not
seated on the ground like a bust of Hermes
at a crossroads protruding in this taken-in
and given-back water to read aloud a line
of scummy leaf-bits sticky enough to adhere,
while all the other runs with whoever wrote
this chair-rail of Tibetan twig-cypher: is,
could, into the going will, does, are,
gone, and here, and there, let remain
as remains, a muck-statue of me speaking
the first verse of its debris song,
that has only the one, "I must stand up
and see what works and what doesn't, start
cleaning, must stand and start, must, must,
can't, must..." and so on the mud-verbs spell
around the inside of the house, everything in it
lonely for singing-breath. Take me with you!
Naked again, and bringing more naked invitees
to the hopeless expungement of wall and floor,
lead us all *out* wherever you swim
your swift enthusiasm, sleek, wivvery,
sunflower seeds of a schooling choir,
deep-pooled under a roaring event-roof,
full-shivering sliders into a nativity
that accepts everything, water of life, being
with known and unknown others under
the force of discourse in sweet community,
and as well paralyzed in a sodden armchair,
and as well, escape itself, scintillae
scattering on a stirred surface, as those there,
the lake-lovers lying on their backs pointing,

become meteors, and Cassiopia slides
through the hemlocks. Sand and small rocks
clog the toaster while dawn down-comes
inside the liquid light-kissing fingertips
lifting the fogfed, thinning juice-door
onto the washed scene. Many voices
in cahoots: am eye am, can tell how the table
puts down one leg before another, and silt
settles from within its ash-fibbling layerage,
can watch the water-inhabiting motion take
other shapes, leave this digression covered with
a fuller's earth of the most unfortunate good
luck to have to have a creek near enough
to rise overhead that now recedes
to a more measured sound, a plucked-string,
fretted and released body, banking back into
an almost obeyed grammar, the patience
and ordinary agreement of rock resisting water,
can hear from out in the Sargasso eel-squirm,
a couple talking, and be both. Pooling
and evaporating eddy-niches expand
to a bland and obvious pond. Forms of
forgetting and waterfalling spontaneity mix
with sky to become the fascination tremendans
coursing through, this coldness my whole head
dips beneath, called Fightingtown, *Un-ul-sti-yi*
in Cherokee, a cleared place, a chief
skilled at village-against-village,
and the quick river that ran in my house.

I invite you in again and again, but you are not
the streaming I long for. You dribble
your drop on mine, and we wed,
wanting greater deluge.

Easter Morning, 1992

A bright copper and brown striped lizard,
big for this area, seven inches long,
has taken over my mop
drying on the back fence.
Here four hours, bent over
like some clearly crazed old man
humping the back of the head of his goddess,
his goddess who has only the back of a head all round.
Not that there's pelvic motion,
but he looks tranced, the perfect five-fingered
hands spread for pleasure and grip.
He neverminds my face so near, nor I his.
It may not look like love but it is
that that keeps us in this head
over head over head, eons.

An Up Till Now Uncelebrated Joy

There's one book, a 1988 volume,
and it's here, never been checked out,
and flipping through, I sniff the carefulness,
the guarded assertions this Oxford guy
spent twelve years considering, so that now
I can have the rest of a Spring afternoon
finding out what's been known and what
will remain secret a while longer
about the Sixth Dalai Lama.

Good scholarship gives me such delight that I kiss
the book alone in the stacks, and I almost kiss
the checkout girl, and I savor the length
of the Bibliography walking through
the self-opening double doors, and I skip
going back to my truck, because Michael Aris
has sustained his interest in Tibetan mystics,

and I want to kiss the bald pate of research
like a n'er-do-well daughter going out on a date,
who before leaving, thoughtfully brings
some green tea for a little break.

Light, Many-Footed Sound in the Leaves

This is what Benjamin heard in the pre-dawn,
studying at his dining table with the windows open,
of the graduate student triplex he shares
with his wife and new child, as he was
mine, as I was, and she, theirs,
a rain of water oak acorns
in no even slightest breeze, overflow
gratitude so early, an elegance,
harpsicordy, to string necklaces of,
and say these are the tiny toboggan people,
much loved and touched, and always losing their hats.
Hello little darling smooth face, forming close
to the mother's throat and the forehead of the father.

Short Prose
for
Specific People

These Things, Hereafter

for James Augustus Pennington

I think the first poem I ever got was one by Edna St.
Vincent Millay that Mr. Pennington read our 8th grade
Latin class in (Good Lord!) 1951. It's called "Afternoon on
a Hill."

> I will be the gladdest thing
> Under the sun!
> I will touch a hundred flowers
> And not pick one.
>
> I will look at cliffs and clouds
> With quiet eyes.
> Watch the wind bow down the grass
> And the grass rise.
>
> And when lights begin to show
> Up from the town,
> I will mark which must be mine,
> And then start down.

I was fourteen at the time and had grown up as a kind
of joyful solitary wandering the Baylor hill. I knew those
cliffs and clouds, and I had looked with quiet eyes. For
the moment, *self* and *world* came together in *words*. I still
like the poem, though the first stanza seems inflated. Too
sticky-sweet for my taste now.

But O, I can still respond to the center of the poem, the
grass and the wind part. There is a phenomenon in human
experience that needs a name. Some have called it the *hieros
gamos*, the sacred marriage, a kind of glistening in the
consciousness. Calm, trembling times when we feel a deep
sense of harmony with the soul. It's part of the work of
artists to find images and expressive form for that.

I'm happily snowbound in the north Georgia mountains as I
write this (Sunday, April 5th, 1987), and hear suddenly the

ten inches of snow slide off one whole side of the A-frame roof. A slow, undertowing sound, almost as though it's inside me, but the dog has her ears up. Each of us discovers different ways of welcoming the universe into us, of being less and less defended against the warmth of the sacred marriage. Poetry became one of my ways. My brother Herb has riding the whitewater of the Chattooga as one of his. That's what the Greek term means. It's something essential and exciting, what I felt in Pennington's class.

Ecstatic, pure-being moments are not, of course, the whole story. There's irony and wit. Reason and clear-eyed judgment, and the grounded ramble of an ornery human voice. There's Pennington's mighty opposite in those years, Jim Hitt. But what I, and others, learned from Pennington were *moments,* and the way sometimes words and the world can sing together.

Pennington could recognize those sacred-marriage, St. Vincent Millay grasses when he saw them shining in a Latin phrase, in the elegant condensation so possible in Latin. When Herb called and left the message on my machine that Mr. Pennington had died, I went to my old Virgil book and opened it at random. Now, there is some precedent for doing this. After Virgil's death it was a common practice, called the *Sortes Virgilianae,* to consult the works of Virgil to learn the future. On and off the practice continued, even into this century. The British High Command consulted Virgil for advice in WWI! (Pennington would love this scholarly aside.)

I open to page 474. It's Book VI of the *Aeneid.* Aeneas is getting a glimpse of the other world! The only phrase circled on the page, in my 1955 scrawly pencil script, is

Hac iter Elysium nobis,

which means, "This way (takes) us to the Elysian Fields (the sixth heaven)." How wonderful and incredible.

This is how it might have gone in the longago classroom.

"Which words did this guy Virgil choose to put next to

each other?"

Silence.

"*Iter* and *Elysium*," he screams.

("Iter" is our word "itinerary.")

"What is he saying!" Pennington climbs up and is now standing on his desk.

More silence. Pennington descends and circles the room, prowling, pulling shirts up, untucking ties. "What is he saying?"

"The trip feels heavenly." Borisky feels brave.

"You would." Borisky's shirt gets unbuttoned two buttons.

"Go for the gold!"

"Hey, take a round off, Seessel, yehhhhhhh."

"The journey is the kingdom." My try.

Long pause.

"You know, Coleman, I think so. I think soooooooooo."

(I was his favorite, some days.)

He sits back down in his tilt-back chair, relieved, and tilts way back.

"Oh young men, I love woids, woids, wooooiiiidddds."

Arms open, shivering upward, "Iter Elysium!"

Over his classroom door, as you went out, was the sign,

HAEC OLIM MEMINNISSE IUVABIT

Hereafter, it will have been pleasant to have remembered these things.

Haec olim. Yell it, HAEC OLIM!

These things hereafter, Mr. Pennnnnnyyyyyyyyyy.

As I look up the Millay poem to check how closely I remember it, close enough, here on the opposite page is another poem of hers that I remember Pennington loving.

Lord, I do fear

Thou'st made the world too beautiful this year;
My soul is all but out of me,— let fall
No burning leaf; prithee, let no bird call.

Such an extravagant heart, Edna Millay, and James
Pennington, in his *moments,* was more than a match for
her.

Rained In, Nursing Unacted Desires

for Brown Leach

When I was five, I got my wish for Christmas, a red
tricycle. I recall the moment perfectly, of going into the
living room and seeing it in the most conspicuous place,
without any wrappings, bare, and directly in front of
the tree. I couldn't look at that tricycle. I went to other,
trivial, presents on the sofa. Then, when it was the
undramatic time, and the others were occupied with their
own unwrappings, I snuck upon that loveliness, took it
outside, and stayed glued to it the entire, cold, unfed day.
As Brown Leach says, that's like the beautiful girl he's
wanted for years, and there incredibly she is, naked under
the covers in his guest room begging in secret whispers for
him to come to bed. Instead, he shuts the hollow plywood
door and crawls in with his wife. *It's the way I am. I
couldn't do differently. I could, but I'd know it was wrong.
I'm Dimmesdale.* What about Blake? Better murder the
infant in its cradle than nurse unacted desires. Better no
half-measures, no near-hit-near-miss timidity? I don't know,
but the truth of my tricycle is, I didn't have the grace of
open delight with my family. Holding back was my way.
I'm given a tricycle, and I won't get on it in front of my
brother and sister and mother and father, who only want
to see my happiness. Is it so secretly inner that it can't be
shared, that joy? Women have taught me to be easier with
that. Friday nights with Ann Corbitt dancing, feeling each
other's skin becoming electrically alive. And the high school
sophomore girl, a last-minute accidental date for a basement
room party, she puts the cool back of her wrist against the
back of my neck, pulls my head down and kisses me like
the movies. Her cool-warm forearm stays wonderfully clear
in my perfumed mythology. Then the day after, and the
week after, she ignores all looks and nudgings. Till finally I
ask her what it *meant.* "It didn't *mean* anything. That was
that night. I just hope you liked it." O wistful lechery, not

important. What matters is to be *present* on Christmas. And these days, June 9th through the 12th, when every time we look there are flowers coming along the creek, little parasols upsidedown without handles. Mountain laurel overhanging the water, letting blossoms go to keep us constantly in the same thought with the light rain: the gift is going by. Here's Brown Leach's food dream: he's standing on a curb, stuffing a hotdog in his mouth, greedily, completely. Then, there in front of him in a slowly passing car window is the woman's face he's been waiting and longing to see again for years. This is another, different, more profoundly loved woman. But he can't speak with his mouth so stuffed. He can't spew the whole mess out on the sidewalk for fear of repulsing her. She waves a slight hand. He, some quizzical, despairing fingers.

Sumac and Lacrimae Rerum

for Peter Thurnauer

The phrase, *the tears of things,* comes from Virgil class,
where we memorized phrases without having actually
gotten far enough along in the six books of the *Aeneid* to
know any context. I still don't, but it doesn't need much.
I don't cry enough. I appreciate those who do. Crying is
fine language, but I don't know what to say back to your
wet face, wanting your lover who's married to someone
else, as are you, and things coming to an end you don't
like. Aeneas had to leave and go found Rome, and there he
sails off with Dido's funeral pyre burning in the distance.
There's something skewed about love problems versus
career, and unexpressed anger hanging around in Dido's
suicide smoke. *Dux femina facti* was another. "A woman
was made leader," And *Fervet opus!* "Hot glows the work."
You want more power in this, maybe, and some work
that tires your body good. I don't know what I'm talking
about. I haven't sat in a car with a woman and cried over
circumstances in fifteen years. But I do have near-automatic
reactions, which may be like tears. For example, when I
start writing on anything, old Latin classes, I switch to
some small something to forgive myself for, my lack of
tears. But then, not quite, I flipflop and justify. Maybe any
sustained thinking moves into shame. As there's some plant
you notice when you take a walk with a friend you see
only once a year, or less, in different parts of the country,
but you both invariably point to the ingenious sumac,
shame. Everywhere, this weedy elegance growing at the
edge of long talking. It comes up in Latin or awkward
English, as it did through four years of class with James
Augustus Pennington. To honor that, picture two friends
and me, sitting on concrete steps with one dishonorable
interlinear translation between us before class, working
through the day's "cuties," as Pennington called the special
Virgilian fancinesses. The grainy rerum made of tearsalt

are everywhere you look, the shame of cheating, forgetting, not doing what we claim to have, but loving language as Pennington did. He cheated too, with his own interlinear hidden away on the shelf by his chair at home. Lots of school was instruction in how to play the charlatan. Truth not much loved, hypocrisy constantly encouraged. But there are still some of us cheaters who savor bitter sumac, and feel grateful when we weep, not knowing why, for the dumb things themselves.

Tree Limbs Overhead

for Bob Bradley

In William Blake's watercolor, "The Youthful Poet's
Dream," the young John Milton, naked and idealized,
lies napping beside a stream. A small sun is setting in the
background. Above him a dream appears within the much
larger, glowing, unsetting orb of his imagination, supported
on the left by Ben Jonson, reading a book, and on the right
by Shakespeare, waving some pages. The dream is "Hymen
at a Marriage and the Antique Pageantry Attending it."
There are scenes inside each half of the globe. On top,
grey, static figures line up on the diagonal as though for
a wedding photograph. In the bottom half, two girls are
doing a flowery fishbowl dance. Underneath the sleeping
Milton, hovering over the stream, three tiny women seem
alarmed at what's going on, faces concerned. Poor dear,
what will he dream next? A solemn, unexplained, robed
man stands with head bowed in the lower left. Leafy tree
limbs enclose the entire scene, indicating, say the notes, *the
opacity of his vision.* I've kept a journal of such dreams for
ten years. Here's mine about marriage, with its pageantry.
It begins on a basketball court. My bride-to-be and I are
playing a new game with an elaborately etched brass *thing,*
like two pestles welded together at their small ends, with a
thick brass ring welded around the joint. The game is not
competitive, no score. I catch it with one hand and throw it
back so it can be easily caught. My son Coley is standing to
one side tossing gold crosses through the basketball net. The
thought occurs during this that I *am* a thought, *the* thought
that will occur to Jan van Eych to put a convex mirror
in the background of the Arnoldfini wedding painting,
reflecting the ceremony from behind and dimly revealing the
painter at work. I am that idea, before he has it! But I am
still also my own physical form, and it's time to proceed
with my marriage. Along the path the way is blocked by a
huge spiderweb. On the horizontal center strand are four

miniature big cats, leopard, lion, panther, tiger. Perfectly formed, but smaller than mice. A giant spider appears from the upper left of the web, descends, and devours two cats. From the bottom right, a mother lioness, normal size, equal to the spider, quickly takes the remaining two cats in her mouth protectively and plops them out safely on the ground. This is a vision of what blocks me? There's a beautiful, traditional patterned quilt hung up down the path behind the web, squaring the circle of it. Two gobbling mothers, one preserving, one destructive, are what I face on the way to being whole. Thick tree limbs overhead indicate how limited my vision. Quilt and guilt, I do love the nightly masque that keeps decorating my blindness, with ceremonies that half-protect and half-consume.

The Phone-Place

for Coley

I picked up Coley from school this morning at ten-thirty.
The school nurse called and said he felt sick. No fever,
but dizzy. Some leftover roast he ate elsewhere last night,
because he loves roast beef and couldn't quite stop in time,
though he knew it was tasting funny. He went on too long
hoping it would start tasting right. It looked so good. Coley
drew a picture of his life once, on rough-grained, second
grade paper: two brother birds flying between houses, over
a scrawly fence. The arching necks of the birds lined up in
the air so full of effort, the smoke from the two chimneys
blowing off the paper in opposite directions. I let him
out at his mother's and get to my eleven o'clock class,
then my one-fifteen. Now it's three, and I'm thinking he's
probably been watching game shows or fixing his bikes.
He's been asleep he says, a couple of hours. Now he's
doing homework, such a dutiful worker. He really did have
something wrong with him. I'd never question that anyway,
or blame anyone for the roast beef, if that's what it was.
We're often wrong about details, but there is a telepathic
love, a region where we wander in and through each other
with shyness and patience and grace. Coley and I joke
around on the phone: hello is this Mayrelle? *She's out right
now. She fell in the hogpen.* Ain't that something? She ain't
so smart, is she. What she been feeding those, you reckon?
Cookbooks. Well I'll be dog. What else? *Dirty clothes.*
He's looking around the room just saying what he sees, so
completely on the phone, in the phone-place. Bud, you're
feeling better, aren't you? *Whaw.*

Sleet

for Harrold Parrish

First calendar day of winter I drive up to the mountains,
sleet-slushy roads, and don't make it, leave the truck with
its passenger-side load of books and groceries and wine a
mile and a half back at a turn-off place and walk in with
one plastic bag of bargain chicken thighs. It's supposed
to warm up tomorrow. Chicken on low, with every spice
and herb I own, smelling wonderful, even red pepper.
Two years ago a poetry student of mine who went on
sort of aimlessly to English graduate school—you couldn't
imagine him teaching a class, very withdrawn and reckless
and sweet—would come to my office and stand around
while I was working, blurting out anything self-consciously
strange and giggling like he did when he read his poems.
Why don't vampires dress in plaid?—has been found frozen
to death in his car. He'd been drinking and passed out
behind his father's house, neglected to go in and get to bed
one real cold night. I've checked out his master's thesis
from the departmental office and have it here in the cabin.
Some service is due him, some notice. Some blame attaches
to me. We used to have a poetry group when he was an
undergraduate. We drank too much red Gallo, and I should
have warned him away from graduate study that couldn't
lead anywhere, that just made him depressed and frustrated.
I've heard he'd been looking for a job for at least two
years before he died. No openings, so he'd gone back to
stay with his parents in Rossville. Everybody called him
Parrish. When you met him in the hall, you'd say Parrish,
louder than need be, and he'd smile and nod elaborately.
His thesis is about the wedding-feast in the Middle English
poem, *Cleanness,* or *Purity,* which was bound in with the
Gawain manuscript. One invited guest to the banquet has
torn and messy clothes, an allegory for the impropriety of
spiritual carelessness in the presence of the Lord. Parrish,
himself famously scruffy, writes well about that filthy figure.

Fallen man, saved, invited to the feast, goes, but in old clothes, still pleased with sinning. The misty sleet slicks and seems to clean everything tonight. Even this near-to-rotten shard of plywood I bring in to burn is a gleaming gift, enameled. Emanuel. In dream recently Parrish was barkeep and keeping the bar open after closing-time to let me have a special beer and tell me of his new love, Jessica Savitch, the newslady. We try to find her address in the phonebook, on *Lila* Drive, and do. I realize that I too am in love with Jessica Savitch and hadn't realized it until now, but I don't tell Parrish and won't interfere. We go to the ridge where she lives where there's a school where everyone learns how to *praise,* constantly honoring the glory of God. Parrish says he doesn't think he has much chance to court her with that kind of competition around. End of dream. One way I clean up is to buy an empty book to keep a weather and other natural observations journal in: December 21st, low 20's. An inch of sleet this afternoon starting around 2:30, misting crystals till midnight, great slender lozenges of ice on the creek, ten, twenty feet long. Midnight to 10 a.m. a warm, Gulf-of-Mexico drizzle comes and makes the ice-sheathing drip and turn loose. Simple notation to balance my dream obsessions. I have napped many a time between towns on the carseat with my pony-express satchel for pillow, sleeping off each successive night's ragged enthusiasm. Learn what I seem to have great difficulty learning: there is a bright-cold sobriety, a steady calm sleet, that includes every possible drunkenness. Don't get tipsy with the wine of beings loving being, that song. More times, wait for clear pin-sounds to touch leaves and grass and railing and roof. In this allegory, cleaning means watching and listening, *tk-tk-tk-tk-tk,* quiet everywhere-noticing, not the celebration-recuperation cycle I've had enough schooling in. Parrish, I'm soberly iced-in with you, my bottles of rhine wine more than a mile away up the unwalkable road, cooking a wedding banquet for one, practicing a purity we ought to have been teaching each other ten years ago. December 22nd—up to 48 at 5:30 in the afternoon, light rain, grey-green overcast all day. Truck unstuck from iciness and unloaded, now stuck again in mud halfway up the hill, trying to drive over to check the mail. Harrold Parrish had sorrows and foolishnesses I played no part in, but I could be a lot more conscious and helpful than I have been. Parrish sleeping into death on the carseat reminds me how important every minor word we have with anyone is. Backsliding, fishtailing, and the road covered with crystal.

The Brain-House

for James Wright

There's a sort of a shed he had built he calls his brain-
house. On concrete blocks, with carpeted floor, wallboard,
electricity. He goes there to write whatever comes. In the
mountains beside a creek, with the creeknoise so loud
you can barely talk. He goes out early this morning,
unhungover, having been a good child to his soul last
night, to write on his yellow legal pad or type on his
Royal, he thinks, but he can't sit still. He feels too good.
He dances some sliding dance steps up and back along the
narrow floor. He sings something he doesn't have words
to, ummmhmmmmmm whumtoopootee poopah, ta. I say
he when I mean myself, or anyone before he knows for
sure what he's dying of, say cancer of the intestine. Before
any symptoms. No tests have been run, no x-rays. He's in
his brain-house so dumb and happy he can't settle down
to do any work, so he writes funny letter-notes to his
friends. James Wright is dying, for certain, these days in
late February and March 1980. Cancer of the lymph and
throat, and mouth and tongue. I've never met him except
through what he wrote. Those ponies he stopped with a
friend to pet one late afternoon by the highway, and the
Sioux Indian with a hook for one hand in the bus station
in Minneapolis, who gave him sixty-five cents to get home
on. Small kindnesses he took some pains to record, because
of the many different ways, he knew, we go away from
each other, then try to come back with a phonecall, or very
like a phone ringing. Now I sit in the comfortable reading
chair I've lugged up to this chamber, and try to begin this
other dance, the one the bright-sun daylight, even if it were
a man or a woman, an old friend standing in the door,
could not see me do. I've heard that James Wright had a
photographic memory. He's been known to stand on a chair
in a small entryway in Ann Arbor and recite the whole of
Byron's *Manfred*. With no one listening much at the party,

but there he is saying it without the book. I learn so slowly
not to be careless and wasteful. Be mindful, I pray to myself
this afternoon, with memories disappearing, detail lost.
My father's recall totally gone, along with James Wright's
incredible *Manfred*. Right after lunch, when we'd learned
that mother had died, Dad sat in his armchair and looked
at me. *I feel like hollering, if I thought it would do any
good.* He didn't, but he did die six weeks later, instantly, of
a massive stroke, as though he could choose to do that. I'm
not one to scream either, but there is a scream inside me,
and a stroke. Knowing and not-knowing, creeknoise and the
other. I would like to get something done in the midst of
this. Throw the camera at where the surf exactly hits the
bottom of the cliff. I want the event and the memory of it
to come even with each other, and there they would be,
standing on the doorsill, together.

Carolina Silverbells

for Milner and June Ball

Out in the meadow beside the house to give coffee water
time to boil, to check closer on the Carolina Silverbells in
bloom that friends identified for me yesterday, so I can say
their names too when I see them somewhere else, here's
a big turtle like a so obviously placed gift package where
I couldn't possibly miss it, right in my no-path through
the tall weeds. The hinged front third of his bottom plate
closes with a wet hiss as I pick him up. Thirty minutes
closed on this wooden table with me, coffee cup and
spiral notebook, he opens a half-inch, puts one back-right,
black-lagoon suit, lizardfoot down, eases his phenomenal,
strong head out from under the eaves. No eyes. They're
thickly cataracted over with layers of film. He tries once
with the back of each foot to clear his vision, like a cat
washing. He does have the clean, minutely drilled, twin
holes of his nostrils. He stretches and points them in three
directions. Now he lunges quickly away from me off the
edge of the table. I catch him. He can see slightly out of
his left eye. When I'm within arm's reach of an animal,
I think of St. Francis. Animals gauge my restlessness. I
want them more comfortable with me than they are. St.
Francis, so empty of fear and hasty nervousness the birds
would light on him. Turtles probably wouldn't slam shut
when he picked them up. I put this one back where I found
him/her — him, there's the small dent in the stomach-plate
for balancing in the act of copulation — and go on trying
to identify Silverbells. Trunk and branches small and
twisty like dogwood. Why learn the names? If I don't, this
place remains a green fog in my mind. I'm told the spirits
sometimes don't know who they are at amateur seances,
when they're called forth by someone not ready to do
that. You ask, "Is this Shakespeare? Aunt Edith?" And the
spirits say yes, because they're in a blurry limbo where they
actually are nobody, and everyone. Names do matter. The

Druids had a tree alphabet, that's been lost, but evidently, in it, each letter denoted the essence of a particular kind of tree. The letter meant that within the silver ash that makes and keeps it such, that within the hemlock, the black tupelo, the white oak. Think of spelling words with those reminders of tree-essence. It's friendlier to have signs for the clear and separate beings of plant and amateur botanist, each living spirit like St. Francis. These blossoms here are white, hanging straight down, little Tiffany Victorian reading lamps. The turtle is out walking again, already, with his misted-over, translucent will, and his lefthand slit of place coming through one eye. I read about St. Francis and trees, and then there's this figuring *work* to be done. I might have thought one time that classifying was distancing. There is some separateness to naming. But past the thumbing through *Southern Trees* to page eight-four there's this Black Tupelo (I think), with me for months, and now I have a term for this presence. Did St. Francis know the names? Probably not. He knew nicknames and spirit-names. It takes so many forms. Studying the differences is trying to join with that clear sap of intelligence, a kind of show-off devotions, while we wait for the true word to open.

On Poetry

for Betsy

The spear-nicks near the bison mean that poetry wants to
take place outside, where there are also spiderwebs: glass
wheels high in trees and hung between telephone wires,
circles as large as you can make with your arms. For five
minutes I drive along at dawn in September and see them,
with a lucky angle of sun and condensation of moisture.
Then the wheels are gone, invisible. I don't know what's
beyond or within this place I think I see. A practice-jab
poem points attention into and through itself, its ignorance.

Fightingtown Creek

for Johnny Thrasher

Five weekends now I've come up here, been told the water's
fixed and five now it's busted, five, or fifteen minutes after
I've crawled up under the house to turn it on, this time
only a quarter-turn, I hear a whang and it's broken loose
somewhere else. I crawl back and turn it off and spend
the weekend again without facilities. I know what's worth
writing about. What the heart, and I know we can't use
that word very successfully anymore to mean the loving the
self has in it, let's say it anyway, what the heart remembers,
what the mind is sometimes so attentive and attuned to that
it carries it in its pocket from then on. Anything might be
reduced to that handy size, the Matterhorn for example, a
cameo of Confucius. I don't deserve to get mad about this
water business. I've never plumbed a house. I call Johnny
Thrasher and say this water's broke loose again. He says
Ain't that a shame. I'll git up ther Monday afore work. He
does good work. I've just got some trashy cheap piping
under there, garden hose he calls it, put in by the previous
owner. *I'll put some PVC in ther fer ye, new fixtures in
the kitchen and bathroom. It's all jist rotted to rust and
crumblin. Two hunnert and fifty dollars, and I'll garantee
it.* He doesn't want to mess with what I've got any longer.
I might try crawling up under there to see what I could
do, after watching him a few times, a few hundred times.
I might buy a chemical toilet and bring in drinking water
in water bags, not take baths and t'hell with it. I tell him,
let's tear it out and go in with the PVC. He's a great buddy
now, drops in a Saturday morning, already glowingly drunk,
11 a.m., with his wife Ruth, whose grandmother was a
full-blooded Cherokee. *Works perfect, don't it. Looky here,
washerless fossets. I tole you we could git it right.* I am very
thankful for Johnny Thrasher. I have plenty other things I
can do here by myself, other than writing I mean, physical,
survival work for the precarious fleck of consciousness that

is this house. Hauling rock in the wheelbarrow to bolster
two concrete block piers that the stream is beginning to lick
underneath when it rises. I can spend the entire summer
hauling rock to make that bank secure. The work here is
watching water, containing it some. The movements and
sound: thrummings exactly like a bass drum, a low dragging
noise like a heavy glass door sliding open. One night I
heard a married couple arguing in the water. Each hour,
at least each hour, I return to the deck and look through
the intricate presence of Fightingtown Creek, named for the
Cherokee chief, Fightingtown. Ruth says, *They's supposed
to be gold and Indian things buried along this creek. Maybe
you'll find something, if you keep digging up rocks.*

Notes on the God of the Cave

for Deborah Felmeth

Les Trois Frères, "the three brothers," is the name of a cave
near Montesquieu-Avantes in the French Pyrenees, because
it was re-discovered in 1914 by the three sons of Count
Begouen. His descendant, *Count* Robert Begouen, hosted the
small group I tagged along with, with such incredible luck,
in July of 1990. Only a very few people get to see this cave,
and for excellent reasons. The images are fourteen thousand
years old and screamingly fragile. One slip, one accidental
brush of a shoulder, and several figures could be erased.
The engraved mammoths and ibex and owls are still damp
in the thin mud layer on the walls. They might have been
made in the last fourteen *seconds.* I kept being told, again
and again, by the kind and learned Jean Clottes, who was
with us, Director of Antiquities for all of France, who didn't
know me from Adam, "You are too close. *Too close.*"
Many of the figures are so small that you have to lean near
to see.

Les Trois Frères is reached by simply walking thirty yards
through woods up a gentle rise beside a hayfield and into a
small vaulted iron door in the side of the hill. Wonderfully
private, like something children would dream up. I felt the
old release inward as I climbed down the first rusty ladder,
release into the cool and the silence, like getting back to
pre-dawn meditation after neglecting it for years.

You change when you enter a cave. You wake inside a
dream, outside of seasonal cycles, outside time. It's very
odd to look at your watch in a cave. The temperature is a
constant fifty-six degrees. Not everyone has this reaction,
but the way I feel in caves is safe, protected, loved, held.
This has been so for me ever since Tom Seessel and Wilson
Cooper and I explored what were landslide caves on the
brow of Signal Mountain. They didn't lead anywhere,
just little rooms, not anything made by the streaming
millenia of waters, but I loved them, as I was soon to love

more the enormous network of limestone caves around Chattanooga. Especially Nickajack. We would gather supplies surreptitiously on weekends, or holidays, and make a day of it. It had to be furtive, of course. No authority, parental or proprietal, could approve these explorations.

Nickajack Cave used to be open to the public in the 1920's. The stream that filters out of it was dammed back then to make a lake that led alluringly into the dark. I've seen pictures. But all that was left of that was the rotted tourist boat and the roofless stone ticket booth and the bent teeth of its turnstile. Nickajack was an impressively gaping mouth, very similar to some of the more famous caves in the Pyrenees, Niaux and Mas d'Azil. The opening of Les Trois Frères is much more obscure, almost casual.

Another sense I have in caves is of being quickened and unlimited. I never fear the lights going out. Other people panic in caves. I'm afraid of heights, but for some reason in caves I know where I am, and how to be there. This is not a reasonable nonchalance on my part. We used to hear stories of men getting lost in the Chattanooga caves and coming out weeks later twenty-seven miles down in Alabama, Plum Nelly. Caves are crawlways between lives.

The highest figure in the rough-rounded sanctuary of Les Trois Frères, which moves upward in a kind of cone, is the one the Abbé Breuil called "The Sorcerer," the one Joseph Campbell named "God of the Cave." He's two feet tall, and well out of reach, fourteen feet up. He presides over a swarm of bison, ibex, bear, deer, and mammoth incised on the stone slabs below him. The god of the cave is instinct and intellect and spirit in one. The full animal inheritance, and the human dance, some inquisitiveness and concern, with a nurturing hunch to his shoulders. A formidable, but not a confronting figure. And the ratio of intellect to instinct to something else keeps changing as I sit in the chamber and gaze—animal, human, god. He will not stay still. Now I see a masked man, an upright human drenched in animal ways, but a person, familiar. Tomas Transtromer has a poem about staring at the cross on the altar until he saw it as a "split-second shot of something moving at tremendous speed." So with this figure caught in a darkroom, developing instant.

This creature does not exist on the outside. He's from the unseen inside. He's something other and something whole, but not wholly other. I don't feel his pieces so much as his presence. He's not a man in costume. This is the one who neither has nor needs tool, book, drum, or belief. His palms are not opening up asking for anything. They are not hands, but paws, and ready for the ground again. He's not bent over in some monkey-effort to stand up and be in charge. This is not a communal person. He doesn't worship. He lives within the union. He is not a static icon, but a being surprised in a moment, the live instant of recognition.

Repose and springy-ness, he has both, and a freedom I can barely imagine. Caving is the perfect "out-picturing" of going within. He is our spiritual nudity, before clothes and all other paraphernalia. He is aware of us, but what else, concerned, hurt, beckoning? I don't know. He's moving. He turns to look. I turn. The interruptedness is key. He's in mid-step-leap-flight, looking over at us, who have for whatever reason come into this motherdark. Why are human beings here? And though he may be interrupted, he's not off balance. He is balance itself. There are no separations in this image. He's the hunter, hunted. Looker looked at.

Powerful, receptive, he may be waiting for us to follow. He's a guide, though the boys' initiation theory doesn't seem right. This feels more solitary and adult. He's humble in his magnificence. He flows with a dancy superbness, quizzical, relaxed. He makes me happy. He's stooping, legs bending and arms reaching forward as one might wading into the ocean. His posture has an underwater feel. Maybe he's a picture of what evolves through the evolutionary process, the invisible moving center. I want to sit and look until I can say *I am that,* the alerted grace of a lion-man-owl-stag-horse-bird being. This dancer is his dance. Joseph Campbell also calls him the Animal Master, with the happy hunting ground stretched out below him. There are black painted flamelike shapes under his hands. What are they? This image is one of the great mysteries on the planet. My reading of what he's composed of is this:

Torso, back, belly, shoulder, paws, mane, penis, thighs, head, ears, face, posture,—LION.

Feet, toes, calves, thighs, eyes, arms, penis, beard, knees, posture, expression—MAN.

Eyes, ears, face, expression—OWL.

Ears, antlers, tail—DEER.

Belly, tail—HORSE.

Some features occur in several categories because they're ambiguous. The space inside the image, the unpainted torso cavity, is very much a bird, a stillness roosting inside him. What is this figure doing? Dancing, springing from one ledge to another, from ground to tree, or is he landing here from above, turning his curious, unafraid but cautious feline-owl head to us? He's very fluid and coordinated. The penis is not erect, but blooded. There is a calm readiness here. He is the wildman awake, a definite *he,* surprised at the far end of the womb where conception begins.

Spontaneity is the feeling. The master at the deep center is pure spontaneity. It's very possible, of course, that I'm projecting onto this cavewall what I want to see, some sufi-zen-taoist amalgam. I don't deny that. Others have speculated that he is an initiatory icon, one to help young males become hunters. This figure, to me, doesn't seem to be about hunting. He's a vision, the son of the great mother. This is the energy inside all creating, looking to see what's become of the dance that curves out from his dance. Bach. Shakespeare. Rinzai. Francis of Assisi. Emily Dickinson. Whoever's crawled in here today. The dance this being sparks in visitants is a mysterious partnership.

I have felt this god of freedom and agility in dreams, sailing in great arcs. Cave-consciousness is eternity. Things don't change here for thirty thousand years. The mud drawings *are* fresh. Daily fears and urgencies dissolve. This has been my experience from 1950 in Tennessee till now in the Pyrenees in 1990. Caves are the perfect metaphor for moving toward the master within. No goal but a meeting of the eyes. What we see in this fourteen thousand year old rorshak is what's in us. I propose a new theory. That this image was used in a second initiation, not the *rite de passage,* but the one that must occur in middleage that transforms adults into elders. You approach him by way of the "chapel of the lioness," a chamber to the right of the small birth-like opening into the sanctuary. In it, a two-foot high, three-foot long carved lioness. Her presence puts what happens in here beyond adolescence.

The other dancing "sorcerer" in this chamber is only about two inches tall. He has a bison head, and he seems to be carrying a bow, or maybe a musical instrument. He's dancing in among the herd, and he's not facing out. His power is of the hunt, whereas the lion-man evokes a more profound encounter, however evasive and indefineable. Change can take place in one to whom such an appearance occurs. There are two poles to the synapse, and both must be engaged.

But what of the artist? Almost forgotten in the excitement, he or she must have lain at a forty-five degree angle painting and carving like Michaelangelo in a slightly listing Sistine Chapel. There is a ledge conveniently beneath the figure where the artist must have reclined to work. But there are nothing but questions about the artist. We have no clues other than the artifact, this black-painted, engraved combination life-form, who may be the first mystical poem, the earliest expression of an encounter with the mystery inside, where all awarenesses blend.

One final note: The shoulder is emphasized. A dark pack of muscle reaches over from halfway down the back to partway along the forearm. Does a flayed lion look like that? Almost certainly the artist has seen a lion being skinned and was possibly wearing the pelt. The lion's shoulder has been an important image for developing the wisdom and humility necessary in an elder.

A child asks is this a scary figure. It is. To some eyes it may look like madness. But more frightening to me is the possibility of living without a strong connection to this depth. The way I feel in caves is mothered. The way I feel meeting the god of the cave is brothered, companioned. This lion-man sees me and I see him. We are together for a while.

It is late afternoon and lightly raining when we come back out into the odd light of the twentieth century. Billions of rainy afternoons formed the passageways behind us, and for millions more they've held the figures they hold this afternoon. Whatever they are, they can't be brought out, except in old mystery ways. We photograph each other in various happy, muddy combinations at the entrance.

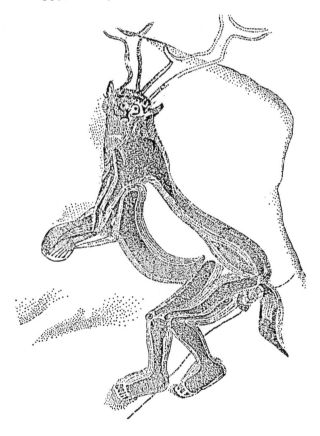

Publishing Myself

for me back then, and Joe Miller

If I had known when my first book of poems was published
with Harper & Row (*The Juice,* 1972) that twenty years
would pass and I would not be able to find a publisher for
a second book, I would have considered myself a failure
as a writer. At least I think I would have. I'm not entirely
sure what 1972 Coleman would have said. He would never
have believed it could happen that way, so confident he
was. He badly wanted a second book out, and what he
intensely wanted he mostly got. He sent various collections
around five or six times a year, all those years. No luck.
Long disappointments are a blessing. It feels very fine at
fifty-five to be publishing my own damn self. I dearly love
the details of putting a book physically together. Typeface,
cover, layout, proofing, all a great delight. The hazard of
self-publishing, of course, is self-indulgence, the absence of
editors to say what not to include, pieces here that in two
weeks, or two years, I'll regret. If I were to publish my
first book again, it would have only three poems in it. No
matter. Twenty years of literary rejections have brought the
keys to the granary: I am in this to connect with mystery,
to walk around and observe my life, to find ways of playing
with what washes through, lichen shelves ringing the dead
tupelo, and I don't know why else. What I felt at twenty,
or thirty-five, about writing was whatever those feelings
were. This now, less manic, more patient and sober, empty
and clearer, more delighted with the limitations of words.
Son-Friend, the taste of truth and beauty cannot be held in
language, nor any unglued, tongue-in-groove, worried surd.

I heard such a voiceless tone from Allan Kaplan, who
also published a book of poems with Harper in 1972.
This was ten years later. He was one of a group from
a meditation ashram visiting my teacher, the sufi sheikh
Bawa Muhaiyaddeen in Philadelphia. "How can you keep
writing poems when you know *this*?" Allan asked me. I

didn't have an answer then, or now. I used to love to chop vegetables in Bawa's room, sitting at great rolled out sheets of wax paper on the floor. Words, carrot woids, add them to the communal pot, stand around talking together with our begging bowls in line, eat the nourishment, and move through the door the other way.

Devotion-sounds have been part of the last fifteen years for me, and at the same time so have the goat-and-dog bleat of these poems. Joe Miller had a lot to say about making your own, unabashed noises. He didn't want anyone stuck in a lineage, imitating some inherited line like a clone.

> Why look for someone to broker your investment in an afterlife, a future incarnation, or some psychobabble time-share on a plot of astral real estate? You have the power. You are the fire. Just as the earth itself has a burning core, so do you and I. That's where the power originates and surges out from, sanctifying, destroying and renewing the phantasmagoric life of the ego. Feel it. Live it from there. BE WHO YOU REALLY ARE! *You* have to do it. No one else can do it for you.

Joe was tough. The Sri Lankan teacher I mentioned earlier called himself an *ant-man,* implying that we're in an anthill of awareness too big for anyone to get an idea of, beyond what we ever thought "purpose" meant, so there's nothing to be ambitious about. We touch antennae with where and who we've been, and in the contact the work, or whatever it is, the love, is moving.

Gourd Day

for Jordan, who helps wash them

About gourds, one thing they say in Blue Ridge is, "It takes
a fool to grow a gourd," and they notice how I always get
a good crop. The other thing they say is that you have to
hard-cuss gourd seed as you put them in the ground. To
get their attention before they'll even consider coming up.
Gourds are stubborn-stubborn. In the mystical poetry of
Jelaluddin Rumi gourds are a metaphor for human beings,
and their rattling speech. If we make our noises against
enclosure long and hard enough, we'll break out and have
some chance to germinate. This is the process: planted in
mid-May, a gourd vine becomes a wildly growing thing
through July. I have clocked one tendril on a wet and sunny
summer afternoon at one and a half inches every two hours.
The entire vine grows seven yards a week. Of the kinds I
know, one flowers white, opening in the evening, the other
yellow, opening in the morning. Where the flowers drop
off, fruit nubs appear and swell and streak and fill with
rain. In the middle of September you bring these heavy
young-uns in and lay them side by side on newspapers on
the daybed, where they can rot. When they get good and
mildew-black with fur, you take them to the picnic table
and wash them in white vinegar, scraping off the scum
with your fingernails, leaving designs. After another month
they'll fuzz up again. Take them back to the table with the
vinegar and hold and wash and caress them like babies.
Then do it again. You'll have dirty fingernails and hands
that smell vinegary and some fine hardshell gourds. People,
of course, make marten houses and soup ladles and fancy
African instruments out of gourds. Some friends brought me
a Balinese penis-sheath that's a long-handled dipper gourd
cut off where the handlepart enters the womb cavity. Me,
I shake them to loosen the seeds from the clump inside
and give them away whole on Gourd Day. Why can't a
person make up a holiday and a way to celebrate it? It's

December 17th, around sunset, with the sky deep winter red, that I secretly tie gourds to my friends' door knockers and message nails. They call me the gourd fairy. No cards or words go with them. Shelled-in, foolish, and hard to get started, gourds don't mean anything.

Translations Available from MAYPOP

These translations were done by Coleman Barks in collaboration with the Persian scholar, John Moyne, Head of Linguistics, City University of New York, and with other scholarly sources listed in the various volumes.

RUMI

Open Secret (Threshold, 1984) — 83pp. $9.00. A selection of odes, quatrains, and selections from the *Mathnawi,* with Introduction. Winner of a Pushcart Writer's Choice Award. William Stafford, judge.

Unseen Rain (Threshold, 1986) — 83pp. $9.00. One hundred and fifty short poems from Rumi's *Rubaiyat,* with Introduction.

We Are Three (Maypop, 1987) — 87pp. $7.50. Odes, quatrains, and sections from the *Mathnawi,* with Notes.

These Branching Moments (Copper Beech, 1988) — 52pp. $6.95. Forty odes, with Introduction.

This Longing (Threshold, 1988) — 107pp. $9.00. Sections from the *Mathnawi* and from the *Letters,* with Introductions.

Delicious Laughter (Maypop, 1989) — 128pp. $7.50. Rambunctious teaching stories and other more lyric sections from the *Mathnawi,* with Introduction and Notes.

Like This (Maypop, 1989) — 68pp. $7.50. Forty-three odes from the *Divani Shamsi Tabriz,* with Introduction and Notes.

Feeling the Shoulder of the Lion (Threshold, 1991) — 103pp. $9.00. Selections from the *Mathnawi,* with Introduction and Notes.

One-Handed Basket Weaving (Maypop, 1991) — 135pp. $9.00. Selections from the *Mathnawi* on the theme of work, with Introduction, Notes, and Afterword.

LALLA

Naked Song, poems of a 14th century Kashmiri woman mystic, (Maypop, 1992) — 80pp. $8.00.

SIXTH DALAI LAMA

Stallion on a Frozen Lake, love songs of the 17th century tantric master, (Maypop, 1992) — 72pp. $8.00.

Order from Maypop: 1-800-682-8637. 196 Westview Drive, Athens, GA 30606. Postage and handling, $2.00 for the first, and $1.00 for each additional item.